Strategy: The Leader's Role

Successful leaders work on their business not in it

Richard Gourlay

This book is interactive. To access the supporting video content for free please see my website RichardGourlay.com/TheLeadersRole

CONTENTS

Introduction 4

Chapter 1   The Importance of Strategy in Business 7

Chapter 2   What is the role of a Leader? 17

Chapter 3   Leadership is about making decisions..............25

Chapter 4   Strategic planning or business planning?........32

Chapter 5   What is a Strategic Plan?.....................37

Chapter 6   The Constraints of Leadership and Management
....40

Chapter 7   The Difference Between Leader and Manager 42

Chapter 8   Leadership decision-making.................50

Chapter 9   Why Do I Need a Strategic Plan?.................69

Chapter 10   The Elements of Successful Strategy 70

Chapter 11   Strategic Tools External Analysis...................85

Chapter 12   5 Forces 89

Chapter 13   Core Competence Model 96

Chapter 14   SWOT Analysis and TOWS Determination.104

Chapter 15   Strategic Selection...............................111

Chapter 16   Strategic Models 130

Chapter 17   The Importance of Goal Setting 137

Chapter 18   What major problems does your business
address for your target audiences?........................142

Chapter 19   What Happens Once a Plan is Created?.......146

Chapter 20   How to make change happen 147

Chapter 21   Summary of Making Change 159

Introduction

In any organization, no matter how large or small, in any field of business, the role of running it is about making decisions. Decisions are either reactive or proactive, either dealing with situations you face or creating opportunities as to where you are going. Being reactive in decision-making offers fewer options than being proactive, but it is the safer option for many leaders to spend their time waiting for reactive situations to occur, where solid facts enable drive reactive decision-making. It is the brave who move into unchartered territory in proactive planning. Either as a fresh start-up with a blank piece of paper or those who understand the value of looking forward to a world that does not yet exist, but may well do so in the not too distant future.

Many leaders work within their confines of their business environment, but successful leaders focus on where there market is going, they look beyond the horizon and they define where they want their organization to be within that future market. Working on your business not in your business, is not a new concept, but it will only just be a phrase if leaders do not actually know how to undertake the process. How can a leader work on their business, if they do not know what they should be doing? They might as well go and have a round of golf!

This book and my video course: "How to take the guesswork out of your business success", are designed to provide the tools and techniques which successful business leaders use to enable leaders of organizations to work on their business rather than just in their business.

What I have found is that leaders who spend their time being reactive are like fire fighters continually running from one fire to another. They become exhausted as a leader and their leadership is defined not by leading their organization forward, but by managing situations from the failure to lead. This outcome of reactive management, of always having to make reactive decisions, requires making forced decisions, often with few options and fewer ideal options. Reactive leadership, glorified firefighting, is most commonly associated with defensive survival rather than growth.

In my experience, having worked with hundreds of leaders of businesses, from one-man bands through to PLC's in both private and public sectors, leaders who succeed in any environment invest their energies in being proactive.

Being reactive, even being good at it, is not a recipe for success in running a business. Every business needs to be going somewhere, it needs to have a strategic plan, a big picture or master-plan (everyone has their own phrase to describe an over-riding purpose for an organization), which pulls it together and provides it with a purpose, a focus and ultimately a plan.

Without a purpose, focus or plan no organization can succeed. There is nothing to pull it together, to do, or organization to achieve anything. Without a plan and planning culture led by the leadership then there is no direction for the organization to go in. The lack of proactive strategic forward planning holds back companies from succeeding in their field. It is not only the most valuable contribution any leader can do for their organization but it is also any leaders' defining role within their company. Businesses are made and reputations built by leaders working on their business to create a viable vision and deliver it.

In my experience, a successful business leader's primary role is to strategically plan where they are going; they don't succeed by solely reacting to events driven by competitors. Success in business requires leaders and leadership teams to step away from the day-to-day existence and focus on where their markets are going and ensuring how their organization can take advantage of those opportunities.

This book is designed to assist leaders to work on their business not in it. This to me is the key role of this book; it contains tools, techniques and templates I have used to enable business leaders to understand and see the opportunities available to them and enable their organization to take advantage of them.

My video course 'How to take the guesswork out of your business success' defines the process in a step-by-step video program explaining these tools in detail. This book compliments that program explaining in detail the key steps, models and techniques leaders and leadership teams need to go through to create and deliver the successful future for their organization.

This book is interactive. To access the supporting video content for free please see my website RichardGourlay.com/TheLeadersRole

Chapter 1   The Importance of Strategy in Business

How leaders define their organizations' strategy determines the direction of the organization and what it will look like in the future. By defining their business strategy, leaders can develop their business growth plan to achieve both their business and personal goals. A leaders' business success is a clear reflection of their success as a leader, and therefore the success of the strategy they have delivered.

The need for leaders of organisations to focus on strategy has never been more important in creating successful organizations. Successful strategy development for leaders requires them to analyse their competitive environment, define their position, develop competitive and corporate advantages, and assess threats to sustaining advantage in the face of challenging competitive threats. This is the most valuable role any leader can undertake, but it is not something, which can be undertaken within one away-day planning day.

This therefore requires a more formal approach to developing strategy as a specifically defined function owned and delivered by the leader, rather than the corporate away day at the end of a year. Remember, no business can be all things to all customers. So many leaders I meet want to be the market leader, but actually you do not have to be the market leader to compete successfully, but you do need to focus on your company's strengths to find a way to differentiate from other competitors.

Being a market leader is actually one of the hardest places to be in any market. Firstly it takes a huge effort to become a market leader, a continual investment in the product or service package, a major investment in marketing and sales channels to gain that position and secondly it costs a fortune to maintain, getting there is hard, staying there is nearly impossible to sustain.

Any brand leader is set-up to be shot at. That often results in having to continually defend a position against existing and new entrants to any market. The effect of this is to exhaust the company of resources, which is why in established maturing markets, where the value is often not in the brand leading product or service but in the whole marketing mix supporting the market position.

To achieve this mature markets often require brand leaders to be part of a global corporate family, where vertically integrated organizations which include large volume lower market placed brands financially support cutting edge leading brands, which act as the product development division of the global corporate. For example the car industry is a globally integrated industry where the cost of launching a new platform is so expense (somewhere around £1billion) that the technology cost must be shared across brands by being able to survive long enough to cover its costs.

For example Toyota Peugeot Citroën Automobile Czech (TPCA) a joint venture between Toyota and Peugeot Citroën to make a range of European cars from a factory in Kolin in the Czech Republic which make the same car with different badges:-

Citroën C1, Peugeot 107, Toyota Aygo

The alternative French conglomerate Is Nissan-Renault also covers many brands, which have their own identity and provide cross support to other brands:-

Alpine, AvtoVAZ, Dacia, Datsun, Infiniti, Lada, Nissan, Renault, Renault Sport, Samsung Motors

Many historic brands are used in emerging markets, such as Datsun in emerging markets such as Indonesia, South Africa, India and Russia

Global conglomeration is probably best exemplified by big German brands probably the most diverse group is Volkswagen group which demonstrates this more clearly than any other:-

Audi, Bentley, Bugatti, Lamborghini, Porsche, **SEAT,** Škoda

This example highlights the point I make very clearly. Just compare the width of the range of brands held within the group. A potential Bentley purchaser is buying a car from the same stable (corporate group) as a Škoda, probably something Bentley don't promote too much?

Why, because the need to be able to fund the development of Bentley and Bugatti requires the revenues of a huge group which can afford the investment in developing that technology to keep at the market leading position. The race to the top is expensive, it is alleged (Economist) that the true cost of developing the Bugatti is about £5 million for each car, although they only charge £1.2 million for each of the 407 cars (and variations, the super sports) they built. That's a huge investment in a 276 mph 8 litre engine supercar, built between 2005 and 2013.

The reason behind this staggering investment in a loss-making product is that it protects the group market position for its iconic brands within the high growth luxury goods global market.

Flagships do more than just raise the profile of premium brands, they allow technology developments to be created, which otherwise could not be afforded while positioning the brand, which drives the trickle-down effect throughout the group of technology and vitally increasing sales. The increased sales throughout the group enable them to cross-subsidise the technology development.

The great value of flagship product development is in repositioning premium brands, whether part of a family / group or as a stand-alone brand. No matter what your brand is or does having flagship products position the brand to target audiences and develop and launch new technology aimed at tomorrow's target audience.

Once defined, your business strategy sets priorities for the company and management team and helps you attract and retain the talented workers you need. Although each department in your company may focus on different priorities to accomplish specific tasks, these priorities should fit within the overall strategic direction of the company.

The importance of business strategy is that everyone should know what the strategy is. I always use the example of JFK having decided to get into the space-race with the Russians "we will put a man on the moon within this decade" the space-race strategy was defined. From that point the USA Government then created an agency (NASA) to develop the technology and people to achieve the outcome. When JFK came to see the rocket and meet the team, he was walking across the huge hanger with his entourage and came across a janitor sweeping the floor. JFK ask the man "What are you doing" without missing a beat the janitor said "helping put a man on the moon". When JFK was being interviewed **afterwards he was asked by a journalist did he think it would succeed, his response was 'yes, because even the janitor knows what he is doing".**

This apocryphal story highlights the importance of a living strategy throughout the organization. Organizations that outcompete their competition do so because everyone knows the goal, believes in the strategy, and understands their role in achieving it.

Most leadership teams have some form of written document, usually a business plan or strategy plan pulling the strategy together into a single document. This business strategy can be defined in either several paragraphs or be written as a set of strategic statements. It is a summary of how the company will achieve its goals, meet the expectations of its customers, and sustain a competitive advantage in the marketplace.

Your business strategy should answer these questions:

1. Why does the company exist?
2. What does it do well and how does it develop those

assets?
3. Which customers and markets should it be focused towards in the future?
4. What products/services should it stop offering, continue to offer, or start offering?
5. Why has the leadership decided on this strategic direction?
6. How are we going to deliver this strategy, what are the steps and measurements towards success?

Every business strategy should be able to answer these simple headline questions. The communication of this message is as important as the document itself. That means thinking about the format, not just to launch but also to keep it alive, so that it lives within the organization and not 'filed' after day 1 and not seen again until the next year.

Looking at these in turn, the most unusual question I have for you is why does your business exist? People always look at me with a quizzical smile, asking why are you asking me that? The answer is not to make money, as Simon Sinek points out that making money is an output not a cause. Too many business leaders focus on making the money, looking after the shareholders, or the other classic, "well without it I would be out of a job". Now all these maybe true, but they are not the reason behind why it exists.

Every organization exists for a purpose, something it is trying to solve, do better, and do quicker within its market. To add real value leaders need to know and define why the organization exists. Simon Sinek uses the contrast between Apple and Dell, they are the same type of company, able to make computers, but you would never buy a phone, tablet or TV from Dell, while you would from Apple. His argument is that Apple exists to solve customers' problems by focusing on usability rather than the technology, with whom they connect so people buy the Apple WHY it exists, while Dell just sells computers.

Why your organization exists can be its history. Rolls Royce exists because the two men each with absolute passion in making cars better, one who had set-up dealership but was frustrated by poor quality met an engineer with passion. When Charles Rolls, the first man to do the double crossing of the English Channel by plane, met Sir Henry Royce, the perfectionist, in the Midland Hotel in Manchester May 1904, it was their shared vision of excellence and passion for perfectionism which drove the reason why they set-up the car company, it is best summed up in his mantra:-

'Take the best that exists and make it better and when it doesn't exist, design it'.

Three years later in 1907 they launched the iconic Silver Ghost, a car of legendary smoothness that completed a 14,371-mile virtually non-stop run, creating 'the best car in the world legend'. (Source Rolls Royce, who else?)

'Why' is an important element, it is the underlying reason behind the origins of the business, what is it trying to solve, what makes you start it (if you did), what is its ethos behind its existence. If you can find and communicate 'why', leaders can build not just a company, but also an ethos of why you exist which can become the mantra behind the brand. 'Why' is the passion which drives an organization's existence. It is the glue which brings the right people into an organization and motivates them to drive success within it.

The second element in any business strategy is to know what does it do well. If you thought my first fundamental question raises concerns with leaders, this one can really cause problems. Leaders always want to tell me about excellent people, customer care, great products, you name it. Their answers often demonstrating that they don't really know what the company does well. Why is this so hard to answer? It is because leaders are either too close to their business; they grew up in it, or conversely too far away, too involved in oversight and meetings or parachuted in, to know what is really going on as to how the organization is adding value. Ultimately, it demonstrates that they have not thought enough about what the company really delivers to its customers.

So here's my alternative question to answer: why do people buy from you and not from someone else? Now that gets a completely different answer, mountains of value added reasons flow out from leaders. But actually it is the same question just rephrased. What you do for a customer, which is why they buy from you, is about understanding what value you add within your market to your existing customers. Often the reason why people buy from you is due to the intangible way you operate, not the product you supply.

Southwestern Airlines is the classic brand in this, they are a low cost airline operator in the USA. But unlike other low-cost operators they reward their staff for making the journey entertaining (see YouTube for endless examples) from safety announcements to other customer interactions, singing, rapping, dancing are all used to make cattle-class air travel survivable. How do they add value? They simply utilize a under used resource on the plane their staff, who are generally younger (low cost, inexperienced, stewards) who have to be on the plane anyhow to entertain however they like (within guidelines).

Knowing how you add value involves complicated ideas, like asking your key and high profile customers why they buy from you in a Business 2 Business (B2B) environment or asking consumers (B2C) what they enjoyed about the product and service. This can be a formal process or just a whiteboard where people can leave comments.

Take those comments and join the dots together, what are they saying, compared to other players within your market? You might be surprised as to why people buy from you, and it will be things you did not realize you do well, differently or at all which make the difference in winning customers. Always focus on target customers, who pay a premium, not just the loud voices who deafen your senses or the budget ones who buy on price (even Poundland, a shop which sells items for a £1) knows the value of excellence in service, layout, good stock, smiling and plenty of staff, not just the price.

The third element of a business strategy is to look at where you are going. Which customers and markets should the business be focused towards in the future? It is always too easy to look at which customers you've got and try and hold onto them. Protecting what you have will mean you will never go forwards, and like a runner running out of steam in the home straight everyone else is passing them, they are going backwards. So if you hold onto who you have always done business with you will be going backwards, as the market moves, new entrants, a shuffling of the deck as to who is where in the brand pecking order will leave you working with yesterday's brands and legacy customers will drive you to become a legacy company.

This brand freezing always sounds good in the short-term and I find it very common when things are going well, directors like to stay where they are. But like a surfer on the crest of a wave you have to keep moving to stay with it, or you are tossed backwards and un-ceremonially dumped in a swirl of spray. The same is true for brands which stay still in a moving market (and they all move), riding the wave is about moving with it, not sitting frozen in aspic looking at yesterday's sales figures and remembering the good old times. 'Remember when we sold X of this, that and the other', when you ask what changed the answer is invariably, the market, we did just not see it.

Leaders who look at where they are with the customers they have are likely to miss looking forward. Strategic business planning is not about looking at todays' customers and expecting them to be tomorrow's in just the same way. Who will be your customers in 1,3, or 5 years' time? What will customers within the market expect from suppliers then? These types of questions raise fundamental questions about the nature and direction and value of your market for the long-term. Answering them requires we look at the drivers (PESTEL and Five FORCES) to understand where the market is going and what will be its value chain in the future.

Coupled with that question is that any business strategy needs to look at what products / services should it stop offering, continue to offer, or start offering? Understanding the product lifecycle in context to the previous question forces a review of everything we do now for customers.

I remember working at Berghaus in 1990 when the market for our products was charging ahead that we had cash cow products (products which made lots of money but were long in the tooth), which seemed to be holding us back from keeping our position as innovators. We were losing out where cash cow products stopped cutting edge new products which leading retailers would source from more aspirational brands. I suggested that we replace all our products every four years as a policy. I could have been lynched, in fact I could have said that Berghaus should stop anyone climbing a mountain and been more popular!

Cash cow products make everyone in the supply chain money, they are the bankable products and services that fund development, but they themselves hold back development, by creating stakeholder pressure to not change them. Brand leaders in any market know that to solve that problem they need to continually be refreshed and upgraded with newer platforms, so the product like the brand does not stand still. That means making tough choices as to when to cut or upgrade products to keep your market position (place) in the market, the one that you want. Review and forecast, plan for change and balance development and retention with the rate of change within the market to keep you, or reposition you as to where you want to be and who you want to be working with.

Communicating why has the leadership decided on this strategic direction is often difficult to do. 'Because we say so', is not an acceptable answer. But showing your research can equally ask more questions than it answers. Once you have fully researched your vision, your strategy and goals to achieve them, many leadership teams think they have done their bit and they can just hand it all over to someone else down the chain, let the management get on with it. But they can't. It is the leadership's role to lead the strategy, to deliver the vision. So communication is vital, and it starts with passion. The leadership's passion, focus and determination to succeed is paramount to the success of any business strategy. That passion, focus and determination cannot be delegated (it's called strategic abdication), only the leadership can deliver it, because they own it and it is their role to resource it and delver it.

How you communicate it will depend upon your organization, but the passion and determination to follow it through, rather than just let it be this month's project will ultimately determine its success or failure. So, it is essential that leadership teams take ownership and commit to each other and the company that they will deliver it. The business strategy should be the measure of success for a leadership team, how they are rewarded. In today's business world reward schemes are now 3 to 5 years in many sectors, from financial to engineering, reflecting the leader's business strategy timeline. This strategic timeframe for rewards supports shareholder and sustainability timetables rather than short-term tactical results focused incentives around end of year rewards.

The final part of any business strategy is the action plan. Often the missing link between aspiration and operation, the plan is what needs to happen, the first step, from getting people involved and engaged to driving change across and throughout the business. The first steps should be immediate and small, so everyone steps forward together and the action plan must answer how are we going to deliver this strategy, what are the steps and measurements towards success?

Action planning is an engagement process and one that you cannot duck otherwise everything you have to plan is just a paper exercise.

Chapter 2   What is the role of a Leader?

The biggest question I get asked about strategy is what is the role of leadership in creating, sustaining and delivering strategy. Strategy is the sole preserve of the leadership of an organization. Strategy development and delivery is the sole role that cannot be either delegated or abdicated.

Leadership is the role of leading people and the organisation towards the vision. Leaders do not lead by title but through their creation, validation and delivery of the vision for their organization. That is where they have the most value in what they deliver to any organization. A leader's primary and fundamental role is to create the forward momentum and to be able to determine where that company is going.

Working ON their business not IN their business

This is why leaders must be hands on in running their business; they cannot be creating vision if they are firefighting in the trenches of their business. Strategic leadership therefore requires leaders to work on their business, not in their business.

Too many business owners see their role as a glorified manager, the decision maker, and the ultimate authority figure. This position of authority and power often drives leaders to become short-term, managing what is happening rather than looking to the future. This 'I see' leads to short-termism in organizations horizons, everyone is looking at todays' outcomes rather than tomorrow's success.

I often see in these organizations a new type of culture emerging, one where the leadership looks to delegate the role of strategy to outside experts, the Delphic strategic planning, sometimes using Non-Executive Directors to develop where they are going or a team of industry experts.

Successful leadership is about putting enough time and energy into working on your business rather than in your business. Successful leaders can always answer the following questions:-

1. What is driving your market?
2. Where is the growth coming from and why?
3. Where do you want to be within that market?
4. What is your business good at and how can it use those advantages effectively.
5. How does your company position itself to maximize success?

"It is not the strongest species that survive, nor the most intelligent, it is the one most adaptable to change."
Charles Darwin

Leadership and real authority therefore comes by being able to lead people to a defined future. That requires a mental approach, which I see in successful leaders to investing time and effort in working on their business rather than being sucked into it. To do this the most successful leaders spend / invest time in three major distinctive activities:-

They work on their business by investing time in understanding the future by:-

1. Talking to opinion leaders from within the industry, innovative leaders who are trying to drive the industry foreword.

2. Research emerging and yet to emerge sectors within their market, so that they can understand where the industry is growing

3. Network with people who stretch them from other industries, creating diversity of learning about what their organization can be, and can look like in dealing with and becoming resilient to change.

These three investments of more than time but real intellectual capital, are what separates leaders who successfully lead rather than those who have the title but are often no more than over-titled managers.

Note the order of the three points, undertaking secondary research, learning from those at the leading edge of their market. That secondary research delivers added value to the knowledge bank and tailored solution finding, rather than pure but unfocused research. In doing points one and two in the right order successful leaders build upon the knowledge rather than undertaking low value, often irrelevant hobby research.

Point three, the one which many leaders challenge me on most frequently. Why carry out research outside my market? Is at the nub of those challenges. Let me explain. If you want to learn about how to make your business or organization stronger then learning how other people have done it through change, how they have created and responded to changing market conditions and introducing new systems processes and technology.

This, what I call diversity learning, is vital for leaders to be able to create successful and sustainable businesses. This investment of time in learning about how to grow and develop through improved networks of business is one of the hardest disciplines, it is where creating a diverse network of peers pays dividends, often the stronger the network diversity the stronger the capacity to adapt your business.

Demonstrating Strategic Leadership

Leadership as Vision

Successful strategic leadership is therefore about leaders setting the vision for the organization, the future model of the business based upon the intelligence you can gather and develop. That vision of tomorrow's market is matched by where the leader sees the industry and how they wish to see them compete within that future market. Coupled to that vision is also setting the core beliefs of how the company should operate. From that information gathering to understand the building blocks of the vision gathering the leadership must:-

Leadership as Decision Making

Leaders must then make decisions. This is always difficult, because decisions are having to be made upon scant and often vague information or perceptions. Everyone making decisions like to have as much solid information as possible, which is easy when you are looking backwards using solid facts, sales figures, production numbers etc. When you are using perception, guesswork and quality assessments of potential confidence, having effective tried and tested processes such as strategic planning tools, see www.richardgourlay.com, enables high quality research and assessment to be undertaken.

Symbolic Role of Leadership

The third and next logical role of strategic leadership is that of leading as a role. This is the most visual and important role in ensuring success of any strategy. It is to be seen as the leader. That requires belief built upon the effective research you have undertaken. Being seen to lead requires that you own the strategy you are delivering. Secondly it means that you drive the strategy forward. This is important because in delivering a strategy you are making changes that will upset the existing order, processes and outputs of your organization.

Change will be met by initially positive enthusiasm, which will change to uncertainly and hostility, then depression as nothing seems to be working, before evidence of success, often not seen by those undertaking the work. So the leadership needs to oversee the strategy and drive people forward towards the next stage or milestone towards a goal. As success of implementation is occurring, those close to the coal face, those doing work cannot see it, so keeping people on the right track and showing them how the strategy is delivering results and motivating them to keep on the right track is a vital role of the leader leading his organisation.

This role, the symbolic leadership role is best explained in the graphic below. This Kubler-Ross change curve shows how implementing a strategy to people will impact them over time.

The Kubler-Ross change curve

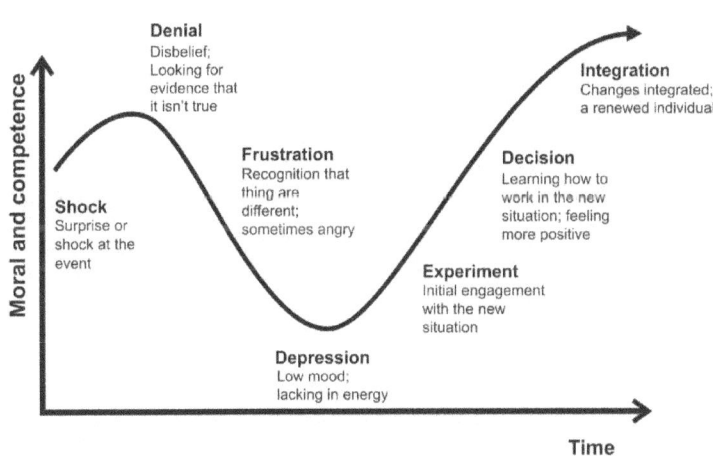

The final role of strategic leadership is about the leader as a command figure. This is the easiest role to identify with leadership and is the most commonly associated role of leadership, but it is also one with a major trap associated with it.

The person in control has to ensure they don't get sucked into the command role. Stepping in is the biggest downfall of leaders. They stop leading and start doing. Successful leaders observe, understand and direct, but do not do. To be in the command you have to be like a conductor (not any or all members of the orchestra at the same time).

Yet many leaders try to help out by stepping in and in doing so loses the ability to command because they are now part of the system not the overseer of the system This role is the one most leaders are comfortable with but because of that familiarity it also means that many leaders feel able step out of the command role to become part of the process and immediately lose the ability to keep in the role of command. To command you must be seen to be in command and see what needs to be commanded. To see who needs help and guidance great leaders need to be able to see not only that things are wrong but also they have to understand what is causing things to go wrong, the cause not just the outcome. Great chefs do not step in; they identify the root cause of the error and then direct people to ensure it is corrected.

The role of leadership

Successful leadership is therefore driven by the ability to create, define and deliver a vision for your organization, which drives it towards the growth markets within your industry or target sectors. While this is the first role of leaders, creating a vision for their organization, sometimes called the 100 day CEO honeymoon period, from the FTSE 100, just creating a vision is only one part of the equation for success.

A vision for your company for tomorrow alone will not deliver results. For a vision to be delivered successfully it requires a combination of resources to be pulled together to deliver successful change and therefore a successful implementation of a business strategy.

Firstly, the role of leaders in creating a vision is to buy people with the right skills. Without skills people will be confused on how to proceed. Being able to get the people with the right skills onboard is vital for a strategy to be implemented successfully.

People also need to be incentivized. Change is one of the biggest challenges I face as a strategic consultant advising leaders. Change is not only painful to develop but painful to implement; why should someone change, move from certainty to uncertainty, risk safety for insecurity? Incentivizing people to make change with carrots and not sticks is an important part of what makes change happen.

If you want people to take risks you have to match them with the right level of rewards, not just financial but also in status and profile in their role within the organization.

For any strategy to succeed it will need the right level of resources, from finance, to across company support and leadership drive. The strategies that are genuinely strategic (fully company wide supported) and properly resourced are far more likely to succeed. Most strategic failures from well-designed strategies are caused by under-resourced or poorly resourced strategic plans, which lead to frustration.

Successful leadership requires effective resourcing, knowing what a company can effectively support and not having too much stretch at any one time. Too many projects put pressure on resources and changing priorities often mean strategic shift as leaders shift their allegiances to what they are sponsoring. This causes people to move to strategies that are better resourced or showing more promising, quicker results.

Finally action planning is a vital element in ensuring that strategies are not dreams or suffer from false starts. Hitting the road running is about getting people involved quickly. Always look for simple buy-in actions that create a flying start and build tangible actions in delivering your strategy step-by-step. Action planning any strategy requires gaining small inclusive steps, everyone doing something that moves them from being spectators to being active participants.

Leadership is about understanding that it is all five key elements, which make strategies succeed. Without the vision you won't get the other essential elements to support your strategic implementation. Which is why creating a vision is so important, because a great vision well communicated will generate the skills, incentives, resources and effective action plan that will maximize the chances of success for your strategy.

Creating Change Needs VISION

VISION +	SKILLS +	INCENTIVE +	RESOURCES +	ACTION = PLAN	CHANGE
	SKILLS	INCENTIVE	RESOURCES	ACTION PLAN	CONFUSION
VISION	X	INCENTIVE	RESOURCES	ACTION PLAN	ANXIETY
VISION	SKILLS	X	RESOURCES	ACTION PLAN	GRADUAL CHANGE
VISION	SKILLS	INCENTIVE	X	ACTION PLAN	FRUSTRATION
VISION	SKILLS	INCENTIVE	RESOURCES	X	FALSE START

24

Chapter 3   Leadership is about making decisions

In all the work I do with leaders in any sized business and across any sector, one of the hardest things for leaders to do is to make decisions. Confident, belligerent and strong-minded leaders say making decisions is not a problem, while those more discerning, reflective and conservative (small c) leaders want to wait until more information is available. It is easy to make a decision which is simple, unforced or the only option, but how often do you see leaders not sure what to pick for lunch. It is easy for anyone to become paralyzed in making decisions, particularly when you have little, imperfect, or no concrete information on the subject.

With hindsight making the right decision seems easy. Looking back leaders can justify their decisions, but it is when faced with having to make decisions about their business, which will impact upon them, their staff and their career, often leaders decide to take the easiest option which is to put off making a decision as long as possible. Let me share with you some of the most common types of leaders I come across when it comes to making decisions, which one is most like yourself?

Decision deferral is such a common leadership factor that many leaders can become highly skilled in being able to defer decisions, just waiting for the right moment, the right inspiration or some magic bullet which will provide them with the insight they need to make the right decision. They start from the point 'do I need to make that decision now, or can I delay it?' Deferring decisions, as a skillset requires the leader to be able to devalue the impact that the delay will have, so that he or she can buy time. This deferral then becomes an endemic trend; leaders can then keep putting off making decisions, with the only damage being the incremental increased damage to making things getting better.

Once the damage is done in missing making the decision when they should have, the pain is only marginally worse as time goes on. This enables the justification which caused the decision not to be made in the first place a life of its own, 'now we've missed the deadline it does not matter as much', 'we are still here', 'things are changing; good we did not make a decision too early'… this self justification for deferral creates a logic in itself as leaders move away from the reason to make that decision, to justifying why not to make that decision.

This decision deferral is a classic symptom, beautifully explained by Mark Twain:

> "Never put off till tomorrow what you can do the day after tomorrow."

Once the slide from making a decision has occurred it is easy to keep putting off making that decision.

Decision paralysis on the other hand is a classic symptom of too much data. Notice I did not say too much information; data is the real problem with leaders facing decision paralysis. This type of leader researches and is hungry for more 'information' They look for more and more sources of information and keep on gathering data, soaking it up like a sponge. As data keeps arriving so it continually shifts the basis upon which a leader can make a decision. This type of leader keeps the door open to those sources and to other additional sources, what the competition is doing, what other stakeholders and consultants keep saying and what the media is saying, just for a small sample for the types of data sources which can drown any clear decision making.

Data is always the leaders enemy. Data is just raw numbers, they are often in what is called 'real time' up-to-date and relevant to what is or has just happened in their business, but they are also the leaders real enemy. Here's why; what is happening right now is the result of what or your predecessor did some time earlier, 6 months to 5 years ago. Leaders have to make strategic decisions, which will drive their organization for the long term. Getting bogged down in the minutia of every detail will drown leaders in making decisions. Data is therefore the enemy as it creates decision paralysis. There is simply too much data from sources in today's business world. From the endless statistics from expensive CRM systems being churned out, hourly, daily weekly etc., through to industry statistics, market research reports, competitor analysis, the sources are endless.

Decision abdicator is the leader who passes the buck for the responsibility in making decisions. These types of decision (not) maker are those leaders who look to find others to carry the can for the decision. In ancient Greece, kings would look to the oracle or seek out advice, on major decisions such as going to war, abdicator decision leaders often do the same thing. They abdicate the responsibility to other parties for difficult decisions. Either through appointing an expert panel to go off and research what options they have and then accepting their recommendations, or by appointing a team (3 wise men analogy) to advise them because they have helped other people make that type of decision in the past.

Both these approaches are abdication of the responsibility for making decisions. Using other people to undertake research or advise is excellent, but the decision abdicator is the leader who does not take ownership of the decision they come to, they have an out, it was someone else's fault. If they abdicate down, creating a working party to devise what is the best decision to make, the working party is being given a poison chalice. If they pick an expert team to advise then they are just abdicating the responsibility to a 3rd party. Either way the decision abdicator is the type of leader who needs to find someone else either to shoulder some of the responsibility for making the decision with them or at worst in taking the whole responsibility for making decisions.

Each of these types of leaders are decision avoiders (and I have worked with all three types of them). The root cause of their behavior is that they are not comfortable in making decisions and their solution is to use one of these types of technique to reduce their personal perceived responsibility. But it is ultimately the leaders' responsibility. They can look to point the finger anywhere else they like, but the responsibility for any decision lies solely with the leader.

Resolving the decision deferrer habits always start by working with them to understand the importance of making the decision at the point that it has to be made. For example I have just been working with the leaders of a high-growth internet retailer, whose leadership team kept missing the deadline for their business plan. By explaining that in not making decisions about where they were going until they were already there they were missing opportunities, which their departments wanted to follow. These included emerging markets, quick wins and long-term profitable market positions. The net result was that key people left, doing anything new was always under-resourced, late and poorly thought-out.

By working with the leadership team we shifted their priorities so that they recognized the vital importance of setting and achieving deadlines in making decisions as part of the process and that the leaders were managed towards making those decisions in good time and rewarded (and recognized) for their ability to make decisions. Stepping into the unknown is always difficult, there is no perfect information about the future, but a decision is more important than deferment.

Decision paralysis leadership is often caused by leaders having worked their way up through technical roles within a company, relying upon data. Develop these leaders to resolve this paralysis is to get them to understand that data is not information, information comes from data but they are not the same. This type of leadership decision-making needs to understand that what leaders really require is quality intelligence. Intelligence is what leaders need and combine not only what the organization does (internal knowledge) with what is happening within the markets (market insights) within which you are intending to compete. It takes a step change in understanding by decision paralysis leaders, to let go of the minutia and think strategically rather than tactically.

Decision abdicator leadership is best resolved by ensuring that they take ownership of what they are responsible in achieving. This requires this type of leader to understand their real value inside the organization. Often decision abdicator leadership is the result of the type of culture within the organization. Typified by the blame game culture, abdicators avoid taking ownership and this maybe the underlying culture in many areas, where everyone is blaming someone else. Where everything is communicated by email, everyone is copied in to everything and senior people are blind copied in. In this type of culture where there are meetings and post event post mortems on who is to blame (the BBC Apprentice with Alan Sugar).

Changing the culture is the only sustainable way to resolve this type of decision abdicator leadership. This can only be achieved if it is led form the top, creating openness and honesty, often new blood is introduced, but if not then the senior leadership, owner and Managing Director (CEO etc.) have to drive that change to a positive culture of sharing, creating a focus on the vision (where you are going), combined with the values of how the organization works (value establishment). Changing culture does not happen overnight but requires linking people's behaviours with outcomes.

Step by step in making decisions.

Types of decisions

Making decisions are part of the leader's and manager's remit. Difficult choices always require a decision to be made, and the way to achieve the fair outcome is to focus the process of decision making linked to the vision and subsequent strategic goals you are focused on for the organization. There are three types of decision in business:
1. Strategic decisions
2. Tactical decisions
3. Operational decisions

The Relationship between Data, Information and Intelligence

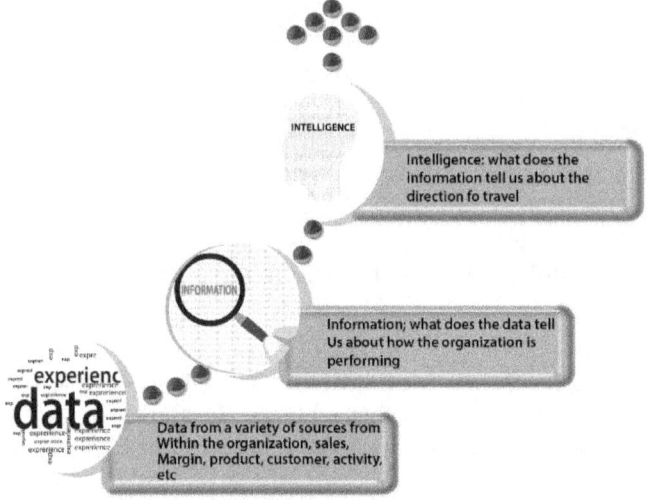

INTELLIGENCE

Intelligence: what does the
information tell us about the
direction fo travel

INFORMATION

Information; what does the data tell
Us about how the organization is
performing

experienc
data

Data from a variety of sources from
Within the organization, sales,
Margin, product, customer, activity,
etc

Strategic decisions are long term, complex decisions made by senior management, the leadership. These decisions will affect the entire direction of the organization; they are strategic by definition, for example the direction to take within the market.

Tactical decisions in contrast are medium term, less complex in nature and often made by middle managers. They follow on from strategic decisions and aim to meet the objectives stated in any strategic decision. Continuing the example in order to become the market leader, a company will launch premium new products/services.

The operational decisions are day-to-day decisions made by junior managers / operational staff that are simple and routine. Operational decisions would involve activities such as how the service is being delivered on day-to-day basis.

All decisions at all levels need data. But not all data is equal, some is more relevant than others. The second important factor about data is that data's value is primarily focused on operational performance. Data at operational decision-making is vitally important.

While at the tactical level of decision-making, by middle management, the data provides the source information. The information, what the data tells us about what is going on, directly informs tactical level decisions and it is information, which should directly impact on tactical decision-making.

Strategic decision-making draws upon a whole range of information sources, which are pulled together to create intelligence. Intelligence, the insights which various sources of information pulled together deliver, is a complete all round view of the business, its current and future market potential.

A business creates a trail of data. This includes data on sales, employee costs and payments. In a large company, such as a PLC millions of data items are created every day against thousands of cost and sales headings. This data can provide a picture of trends, which the business can use in its forward planning. The conversion of data into information allows us to identify trends and map progress against set targets, key performance Indicators (KPI's).

Typical data sources include sales data, turnover, margin, conversion performance and all the measures through the sales and marketing funnel.

Marketing data can overwhelm any organisation; the range of sources can include everything from website hits, to event attendees at shows. Engagement with customers at every level produces marketing data, which can be used as the first part of the information gathering about new markets, emerging trends and existing customer behaviors.

Financial data use recorded data to prepare the accounting statements for a business. Every company (large and small) has a duty to keep accounting records and must prepare annual accounts that report on the performance and activities of the company during the year.

Chapter 4   Strategic planning or business planning?

One Frequently Asked Question about strategic planning concerns the differences between a Strategic Plan and a Business Plan. This is one of the key leadership confusions which leaders face, they want to update their business plan when they should be developing their strategic plan.

The key difference between a strategic plan and a business plan is that the strategic plan is designed to internally drive the organization forward defining and articulating how the business will go forward to achieve the goals and objectives which lead towards the leaderships vision for the organization. A business plan, in contrast, is fundamentally an externally developed document to explain how the organization operates and functions.

The key differences between strategic planning and business planning

The key differences between strategic planning and business planning

Strategic Plans:
a)   A strategic plan is an overarching plan that sets the strategic direction of the organization enabling it to achieve its vision.
b) A strategic plan should be the primarily internal planning tool, although it may be shared with users and external stakeholders.
c)   It can be used to motivate, inspire and lead staff, stakeholders, customers and other parties, and to communicate the future direction of the organization to users and funders.
d) A strategic plan can therefore lend itself to a range of presentation formats. Organisations can choose the format that best reflects their culture and approach.
e)   A strategic plan can provide a basis for more detailed planning including business plans, marketing strategies and funding strategies.

On the other hand a Business Plan:
a) Is an externally focused document that provides more detailed information on the proposed development of an organization, and is likely to be shared with potential investors - funding bodies for the voluntary and community sector.
b) A business plan will usually include more detailed information on the financial position of the organization, financial forecasts, and competitor and market analysis.
c) A business plan is formal and detailed in its structure and contents and is not designed to be shared with employees or target audiences.
d) It may be more difficult to present the level of detail required within a business plan, it is designed and should be written for a different purpose, typically external funding.

The strategic plan.

A strategic plan should tell an interesting story, explaining where you are now and how you got here, explain where you are going and vitally explain why you are going towards that vision of the future and articulate what those goals and objectives are and how the organization will achieve them.

The contents of the strategic plan should relate between 1 to 5 years period of **future** development, depending upon the rate of change of your business sector. A strategic plan is defining to the audience to imagine, see and understand the vision. However, the vision that the plan describes must be based upon the research of the market information gathered from the work which has been undertaken.

How to engage with your team with a strategic plan is an important element of ensuring its success. I recently was working with a global engineering company and its global vice president turned up and just talked about his life and how he had made it to the top. While an interesting story to explain his motivation and route to success, the talk titled 'our strategic future' was more a series of grey slides which inflated his role rather than motivated the audience. He talked about living the non-domiciled life in Switzerland, flying around the world and making big decisions.

This is a typical problem in failing to articulate the future by focusing in this case on the personality of the leader rather than on where they are going and why, the opportunity to engage and involve key staff is lost.

The lack of being able to articulate why an organization exists and where it is going and why is vital to be able to articulate the strategy and direction of the organization.

Bringing a Strategic Plan to Life

The leadership also needs to find the right 'tone of voice' which actually speaks to the target audience. This will help them to see things from the organization's point of view.

This needs to be coupled with the right way to launch the strategy, to visualize it and define it. A strategic plan needs to live, it needs its own identity, and life of its own to standout and deliver the new strategy to target audiences. A strategic plan must also be a living document; it needs to bring the strategy to life for audiences.

The structure of a strategic plan

1 Introduction - the link between the representative of the organization and potential audiences, explain the RELEVANCE
   a) Make it personal to the audience
   b) The leadership must demonstrate commitment to the strategy
   c) Ensure that it is the long-term integrated strategy of the organization.

2 Executive Summary - this is a two page summary of the strategic plan which captures the essence of the organization and what it is going to achieve. Explain the

WHY

3 The summary should include:
   a) The values, of the organization
   b) Long term aims, goals and objectives
   c) Info and acknowledgments re: the planning process, the RATIONALE

   d) The more detailed information that may be necessary for potential or existing funders, customers, strategic partners, builds on the Executive summary and is the HOW and WHAT.

4 Mission and Vision Statements
   a) What does your organization do – its mission
   b) How it does it - your values
   c) Why it does it - your vision

5 The Organization:
   a) History
   b) Key stages of development
   c) How it sees itself
   d) How it wants others to view its work.

6 Critical Success Factors and Strategies - this section should be based on the environmental analysis as well as the internal and organizational issues which have been identified.
   a) Key measures of success (CSF's)
   b) What will tomorrow's landscape look like while explaining what needs to change.
   c) What the strategies are and what they will deliver.
   d) How those strategies will be realized

7 Aims and objectives - the goal-setting and action-planning section, which should explain how aims will be realized in practical terms, and how their progress will be monitored.
   a) This section should outline and detail for each separate project area if the programmed activity is extensive.
   b) The action planning should also demonstrate how the

required changes will be introduced

8 Management of the strategy - another key perspective on the organization's strategic and operational planning.
   a) Explaining the detail (SMART – specific, measurable, achievable, realistic, timetabled)
   b) Ownership of strategies by department and boss

9 Appendices - this section can contain further detail and evidence to support the contents of the strategic plan. Some audiences may need this level of detail, using appendices or subset plans provides all documentation options for readers.

Chapter 5   What is a Strategic Plan?

A strategic plan is a living document used to communicate with the organization the organizations goals, the actions needed to achieve those goals and all of the other critical elements developed during the planning exercise.

It is the most valuable and important part of what any leader of any organization does. The process of deciding strategically where you are going, your vision and how you are going to get there, your strategy is all about taking your organization from where it is today to where you want it to be in the future, 1,3 or 5 years from now, depending upon how fast your market is changing. Your strategy is your direction, which determines where you are going to be as an organization.

Having a strategic plan is having a clear direction you are taking your organization towards.

Having a clear strategy enables a leader to take ownership of their organization, move beyond merely dealing with events as they happen. If you do not have a strategy to lead, then others cannot follow, and so a leader is left 'managing' day-to-day events. They become only able to respond to the competition rather than setting the agenda for driving their business.

A strategic plan takes the opposing view. If you want to be successful then define what success looks like. A good strategic plan is about defining where you are, where you want to be and then defining how you will achieve your goals towards your vision.

One of my clients provides insurance financial solutions to customers. When I first met them they sold everything to everyone they met. They had a wide range of customers with great retention but lousy margins. No real sense of what they were doing or how they were adding value. They were losing money and spending their time managing their existing customers.

They called me when a key customer asked them why they were in business?
They had no strategy, they had no direction, they were loosing good staff and they were fighting just to keep their existing customers. In a market that was rapidly going online, wiping out large sectors of their existing and potential customers.

If you cannot see a strategy, then it is probably because it does not exist.

By defining with them what they were good at, looking after customers, we were able to focus on who would value those services most, high net value customers. By looking at the market, that is where this industry is growing (it has gone online for the low price / low value customers / transactions) there was an opportunity to add more value to high value customers by playing to their strengths.

By creating a strategic plan their strategy has become to focus on high net worth customers, who value and would benefit from bespoke solutions to match their complex needs. This enabled the company to focus on high value closed markets accessed through 3rd party channels such as celebrities and sports people.

By focusing the company's resources on these high value segments, all processes and value added activity was re-engineered to support this strategy. This reduced the number of processes by over 50%, shortening low value time and enabling more resources focused on adding value to winning valuable customers.

By focusing on the growth sectors this business was able to turn the business around within a declining market, which on the surface of it is an unusual outcome to achieve. The reality is that even in declining markets, driven by online low cost alternatives which are dramatically changing that market, there are areas of growth, specifically with those who have needs which are specific and not met by low cost online providers.

A strategic plan drives thinking in 2 key ways, firstly strategic thinking is about looking at what opportunities exist and where to focus to get to where you want to be and by driving changes which orientate everyone towards those goals. Rather than looking at what is happening and seeing it slip away, by focusing you and your team's efforts on where you want to be you orientate and motivate the team towards those goals. Secondly, by standing back and looking at the 'what you are good at' a strategic plan plays to your strengths, where you add real value to customer segments. In doing so you achieve the ability to set the direction you want to take to win, the idea that Sun Tzu first identified when he defined strategy as a military concept.

Chapter 6   The Constraints of Leadership and Management

The key role of management is to deal with the triple constraints, which limit / constrain every manager. These constraints are the limitations of resources available to any manager, time, cost and quality. Every manager has to work within these constraining factors.

Each factor is related to each other in undertaking any work task for managers. So management is about balancing and managing these three resources against the set expectations stakeholders have. Successful management is about balancing these three controllable and negotiable factors.

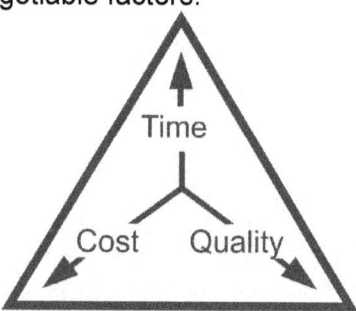

Management is therefore about pushing people to do things, allocating these scarce resources to them to enable them to achieve outputs. This is the push role of management.

Leadership by contrast is rare as a skillset. It is about leading people towards the leader's vision. Rather than pushing people, it is about pulling people, people who share your vision, passion and buy your enthusiasm

The key difference between leadership and management was explained by Eisenhower to his general very succinctly during the planning for D-day in the second world-war, when he described putting a pile of chain on a table and asking, "If I push it which way will it fall?" The generals all gave differing answers, to which he replied, "We don't really know, but if I pick up the chain by one end and walk this way, then we know which way the chain will go!"

Leading is about taking people with you rather than pushing them. As Simon Sinek points out if you pay people to do a job then they will work for the pay, if people will work for you because they believe what you believe then they will follow you because of who you are and where you are going. If you can lead through your authority, your vision, focus and passion then leaders can lead people because they led rather than because they are being pushed.

Chapter 7   The Difference Between Leader and Manager

The leader role compared to the manger role is one of the classic questions I deal with in working with businesses of all sizes. The challenge is that all managers aspire to be leaders even though the roles are poles apart and non-complimentary.

In many businesses senior people are both leaders and managers and understanding how to differentiate these two distinct roles is a real challenge, particularly within smaller companies. In smaller organizations senior people often struggle to deal with the differences in the roles of manager and leader because they are one person working with the same people doing two different roles. How do you wear the same hat, sometimes in the same meeting and yet undertake two different roles, leading people forward and managing what they are doing?

This problem also extends to larger organizations where mangers are promoted to leaders without any real change in the role, no personal development or little role redefinition. Companies too often think that a new job title, a better office, a press release and a pay rise make a leader, then they wait to see how they cope, or fail before helping them to make that transition.

Leadership and management must go hand in hand. They are necessarily linked, and complementary. Any effort to separate the two is likely to cause more problems than it solves.

The leader's job is to inspire and motivate. The manager's job is to plan, organize and coordinate. In his 1989 book "On Becoming a Leader," Warren Bennis composed a list of the 12 key defining differences:

1. The manager administers; the leader innovates.
2. The manager is a copy; the leader is an original.
3. The manager maintains; the leader develops.
4. The manager focuses on systems and structure; the leader focuses on people.
5. The manager relies on control; the leader inspires trust.

6. The manager has a short-range view; the leader has a long-range perspective.
7. The manager asks how and when; the leader asks what and why.
8. The manager has his or her eye always on the bottom line; the leader's eye is on the horizon.
9. The manager imitates; the leader originates.
10. The manager accepts the status quo; the leader challenges it.
11. The manager is the classic good soldier; the leader is his or her own person.
12. The manager does things right; the leader does the right thing.

The leaders role is therefore fundamentally about making the organization fit for the future. That includes challenging where it is going through organic growth (responding to the market) by establishing their vision for the organization, and ensuring it is competent to compete in tomorrow's market.

Conversely the manger is focused on delivering todays' plan. The manager's role is to be efficient and effective as an operational body. Good management is about delivering key performance indicators (KPI's), which reflect operational excellence. I often use the example of an infantry platoon to explain what that means in practice. The commanding officer is set with the task of taking the platoon forward (the leader) while the sergeant's role is to keep the platoon together and maintain its focus on what it is doing (manager). I use this example to explain to people the fundamental differences in the roles which leaders play compared to managers.

The leaders role is therefore to challenge all the assumptions regarding what the organization does today, will they be relevant in tomorrow's environment. Leaders are the owner of the strategy leading toward their vision, while the manger's role is to focus on the effective delivery of the plan.

These distinct horizons, today and tomorrow are important

differentiators in the role someone has, and I think reflect better someone's role rather than their job title in an organization.

How can someone be both a leader and a manger?

Leadership and management are therefore very different roles, but successful managers aspire and expect to be made leaders. In small companies and organizations the same senior person often has to be both leader and manager simultaneously.

Wearing two hats is one approach, but which one fits the person best is always the most important first consideration. As a senior person playing to your strengths is always the most important aspect of the skill set you have to perform. Leader's skills are appreciated and valued as people who can focus on the strategy and the goals that demonstrate progress of that strategy. Managers are often measured by how well they manage people, and the outputs of those people's activities. To do both simultaneously is therefore not compatible but neither is it impossible to achieve. The balance is to be able to switch hats effectively, where and when do you need to undertake either role. The challenge is that as these roles are a very different skill set and anyone who has been promoted to either position has got there by being recognized as good at one how do you balance them up, rather than just overplay the one skillset (the one you are good at) to cover up (offset) the deficiencies in the other. Couple this tendency with the lack of formal training in leadership skill development and the end result is that managers play at being leaders and rely upon either their personality or title to cover over their lack of leadership skills.

The net result is that too many managers promoted to leadership roles have and do not invest enough time or energy in developing the key attributes of leadership, working on their business rather than it in. Many leaders like to be part of the team today, rather than:-

• Know where your business is within your market.

• Know your market and its external and internal drivers.

• Defining and visualizing where you want to be based upon:-

1. Aspiration – of the leadership team.
2. Competence – of the organization
3. Stakeholder - meeting their expectations

- Ultimately leadership is about creating and communicating a clear VISION: ONE WHICH YOU OWN.

For a manager to become a good leader they have to first let go of being a manager, not just the boring and unattractive administration element of that role, but the whole role.
The most effective way to achieve that is to replace yourself in your whole role, make yourself unemployed in the manager role. I often see senior managers shocked when I say they need to sack themselves to promote themselves. If you can't or won't sack yourself then in reality you will never be able to take on the new role of leading your organization.
The key difference to me between a leader and a manger in my book is that a leader works on the business not in the business.
So by sacking yourself, making sure that the business can operate without you, you can then work on it, making it better, stronger and fit for tomorrow's market by being objective and not subjective.

Many leaders I work with get sucked into their business, it always starts with something small, but before they know it they are doing a range of low value work, often someone else's, which takes up their time and even more importantly their energy.

One technique I use is to ask leaders to identify what they do everyday compared to the value they deliver. True leaders ensure they focus on the high value work; they deliver and create clear boundaries as to what they do and what they don't.

Value the work you do as a leader?

Leadership : High Value
Work

Management:
Medium value
Work

Operational
Activity:
low value
work

This model is a simple way to review what you spend your time
doing at work in your business and help you identify when events
pull you into the wrong role. Simply put a value per hour on the
vertical axis for each role and then look back at what you do in a
week, by listing out what activities you did scored against the level
they are at, then you can easily see how you are pulled out of your
leadership role by events.

If you are doing both roles, being a leader and manager at the
same time, I always get people to wear two hats (not real ones,
unless you want to), one for each role. When doing either role you
have to make sure that you know which one you are doing and
think, act and review as that role in either position.

Red timing the role as a leader, if you are mainly a manager, or vice versa, is an essential element in successfully combining these two polar opposite roles. Being able to know which one you are doing is an important skill, compartmentalizing what you are doing and not being distracted is vitally important to ensure success in both.

The most common failure I come across is that of becoming a researcher into a market. Getting carried away with the role of research, in working on it, which can eat time and drag you away from the role of effective research. It is very easy to become a highly paid researcher, justifying evidence gathering, an immeasurable activity to working on your business.

There is always a self-justification in undertaking further research, anyone looking into the future is never going to have perfect forward information, in looking forward I define that if you are 60% sure then that is as good as you can get in looking beyond the horizon. Any more than that and you are either procrastinating in making a decision or carried away with the research process.

Berghaus Case Study – Strategic leadership decision.

I remember when I was at Berghaus suggesting that we should replace all our existing products every few years and even looking at doing that quicker with our flagship product range if we wanted to continually develop our position as market leader. My argument being that developing innovative products which challenged and drove the top end of the market would continually drive the brand's position to be number one in its chosen markets and would enable it to enter and dominate new markets.

The opposition I received, effectively open hostility, from those with vested interests in maintaining the status quo was deafening.

They wanted to benefit from what we had created, either in factory and supply efficiency, who could make existing products effectively and therefore at lower cost or at the other end of the process certain sales people who had bankable orders in their markets who were concerned that changing products they would risk losing customers. This is the challenge, do we do what the managers want to make short-term gains with better margins and certain orders, but accept the risk of degrading the long-term market position in existing markets and limit the ability of the brand to enter new and emerging markets at the right position in the short-term?

This is a classic challenge; when does a business or any organization decide to make a change to what it is doing? This often reflects the internal power of stakeholders and their short term needs compared to the leaders desire to develop their organization forward.

Berghaus at the time operated in 35 markets and was the brand leader in its home market within the UK, and northern Europe, was making in-roads into other European markets, but each was small and fragmented, reducing its opportunity for scale of return to enter these markets. Not an ideal position for sustained growth as each one was small and costly to run.

The brand had also invested heavily in creating technical leadership of the industry without being able to recuperate that investment so the pressure was to create stability, so the decision was therefore taken to retain existing products rather than replace them. This real-world outcome, compromising the position of the brand in the short-term for financial stability created consequences in being able to enter new markets and to sustain its position within its existing markets.

Chapter 8   Leadership decision-making

Leaders have to make decisions.

"The hardest decisions for leaders are the ones not with the fewest choices, but the ones where there is the least information."
Richard Gourlay

Strategic planning leadership requires leaders to step outside their comfort zone and make decisions about the future direction of their business, often on fairly limited, vague, incomplete and conflicting information. The vagueness or uncertainty of information encourages leaders to duck / avoid and delay decision-making. If leaders have perfect information they can make perfect decisions, but only if leaders feel empowered to lead. If not, then I often see leadership adopting one of the 3 classic positions of deferral, denial or abdication in making decision making on their forward strategy.

The propensity of leaders to duck the big decisions in vision and strategy is a major challenge in business success today.

While there are clear cultural impacts around empowerment due to differing cultures (to read more about cultural differences can I recommend: Hofstede's cultural dimensions, for more about cultural empowerment), and the impact upon cultural background, particularly in global business environments on leadership strategy and decision-making. The impact of culture on decision-making is an emerging issue as the world moves east and smaller as barriers come down, we see the emergence of truly global companies.

This change means that leadership of any company can now come from a far wider range of cultural backgrounds. As historically western companies find their growth is coming from the east, particularly China and the rise of middle eastern economies and conversely manufacturing companies founded in the east from the east namely South Korea and China now compete globally as true brands rather than manufacturing labels, as these converge so their leadership can emerge from anywhere.

Malcolm Gladwell in 'The Tipping Point' eloquently points out how differing leadership cultural backgrounds can have dramatic impact upon how they operate. While companies may have operated globally, until very recently their leadership had come from the company's origins. Very rarely did a company pick its senior leadership, particularly its Chief Executive from outside their cultural border, a silent stakeholder requirement, but something, which unlike the race to equality of sex in the workplace, has not been focused upon as to its impact upon company's strategy.

Cultural background itself creates challenges for organizations as they adapt to incorporating multicultural talent within their global leadership. What culture any global organization adopts, is not easy to determine. Many established or merging organizations spend much time and effort defining how they should operate in a global market.

I recently worked with an American multinational engineering company that was struggling to penetrate the culture in the Far East. This was highlighted with a series of examples the best of which was when a major meeting which had taken over 6 months to set-up with the target clients senior management team, ended in complete failure.

During their presentation, the young American led team was being continually interrupted by one quiet man's phone ringing every few minutes. The young American Exec presenting through a translator to a room of people who were all taking notes and conversing, he asked through the translator to ask the quiet man to leave.

Suddenly the room went silent and everyone else walked out. He had just thrown out their Chief Executive.

Their real challenge was that their culture of American Prep look and organization of young blond, chino wearing exec's did not fit with the expectations to their industry globally. The market and client expected senior people, with experience of engineering to be the lead. Likeminded and authority matched people doing business together. That meant job titles that fitted with the hierarchy and social status that came with maturity that complimented complex engineering teams.

My solution for them was to explain how different cultures worked globally, based upon Hofstede's principles. Rather than have preppy salesmen trying to make complete sales process, we established job titles and roles using multi skilled teams, which reflected expectations and structures of their target audiences. This enabled them to speak the language of the industry globally, rather than relying upon an American approach. The difference shortened lead times to get to decision makers and enabled their win rate to increase significantly.

The use of an external party helped them to spot the obvious, they were not making in-roads, but being able to see not just the problem, but the required solution and how they needed to change to reflect the cultural requirements, in people, processes and titles.

The challenges of working globally, using outsourced global services or global manufacturing are understood, but as globalized leadership brings new challenges for organizations most noticeably in areas such as services, digital and software. This new type of global organization is in rapid growth and works without borders and with a new educated online audience. Culture has a huge impact on how organizations deal with decision-making and within new economies as they merge and differences emerge in different ways.

Organizational Culture

Cultures within organizations have a huge impact upon the confidence with which leadership can be delivered. The culture within any organization is first and foremost the responsibility of the leadership team. Most overtly in new start-ups the leadership can set the culture from the outset. From establishing the real underlying vision and values and purpose (mission) of the business, the theory and principles of the organization; through to the more tangible evidence of the culture, how the leadership actually behaves in day-to-day actions and decision-making processes really matter in defining the organization's culture.

In established organizations, existing leadership has the opportunity to mold the culture they want to see, often by benchmarking others they admire or by making leaps through new structures and premises. Existing leadership will always struggle to make significant movements quickly in culture, reflecting the difficulty in leaders becoming something different.

The most effective way to make big culture shifts is always to bring in new blood with new ideas. Without that opportunity, culture shift often takes competitor (or customer) pressure to drive activity. Being too close to something means you cannot see the need for change, a little like aging, day-to-day you don't see the aging process, the same is true with organizations. It is easier to be where and who you are than to move somewhere you do not know or cannot see.

For new leadership teams, the chance to make a shift in culture is often essential; it is part of why the new team has been chosen. New leadership teams have around three months, to determine what their plan is, (see the100 day CEO role) this is the window which typically new CEO's of PLC's are given to come up with their plan and is a very useful point to remember if you are appointed to a new role as CEO, don't jump in and make changes on day 1 (unless you absolutely have to) step back and see what you have and what you need to have before you make the change you want to. Remember the eternal adage:

"You only get one change to make a great first impression!"

The challenge to good decision-making is not just to feel empowered (supported) in making the decision. The other factors, which enable good quality confident decision-making, not only include information quantity and quality, but also the leaders need to be organized as a key skill-set. Leaders who are continually multi-tasking, spinning many plates simultaneously, particularly when they are involved in operational activity, managerial activities and leadership activities simultaneously. Being organized is not only the ability to compartmentalizing and focus on what you should be focused upon as a leader, where you are going, but also the ability to ask the right questions at the right time.

When making decisions across the organization leaders often are dragged into the business and so cannot work on their business if they are stuck in their business. This drag into their business clouds and confuses many leaders, as they become what are so often called 'hands-on' leadership. Being dragged in, to either managerial activity / politics or operational detail is often a reflection of where the leadership has come from within the organization or it is the misunderstanding of how the leadership provides real value to any organization; seeing, understanding and leading it forward.

In making decisions leaders need to be logical in their approach. That does not mean they cannot make decisions based upon emotion, but good decision-making relies on a systematic approach, which provides the leader with self-confidence and supports a process that in being transparent colleagues and stakeholders can see, support and consult with the leader on their decision makers.

Being both logical and systematic, the decision-making process helps leaders deal with the critical elements that result in a good decision. An organized approach enables leaders to be less likely to miss important factors, and enables them to turn data into quality information and subsequently valuable intelligence throughout the approach to make decisions better and better.

There are five steps to making an effective decision:
1. A constructive environment.
2. Generate good alternatives.
3. Explore these alternatives.
4. Choose the best alternative.
5. Communicate your decision, and take action.

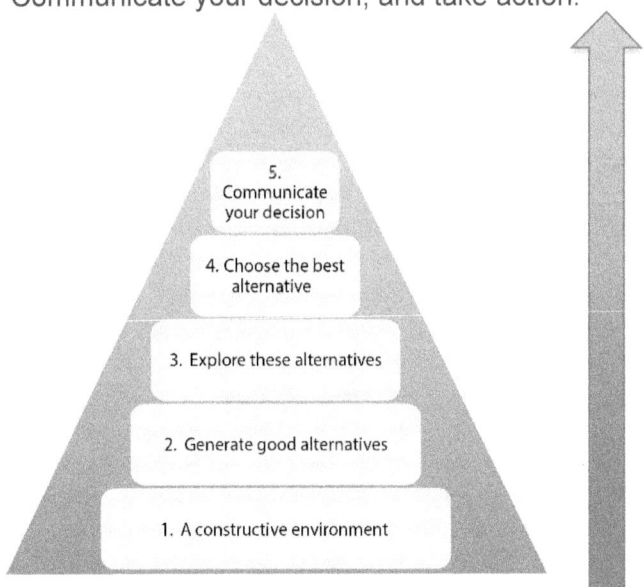

Step 1: A constructive environment

For any decision to be successful it needs an environment, which supports positive decision-making. Positive environments are those where people feel that they can make decisions without fear of recriminations. In a culture of fear, sticking your head above the parapet is actively discouraged, discredited and often seen as career limiting. In these types of environments any project can be undermined and any perceived failure of the project tars the sponsor leadership team damaging its current and future credibility.

For decision-making to be successful the right environment for strategic decision-making to succeed requires that a **clear objective be established**. This is why businesses and organizations with clear visions have clear goals and by being more focused create a positive environment in which they work. Pulling people together towards goals is an integral facet of constructive business environments; they have a purpose and a clear direction.

In creating constructive environment leaders must also agree on the process they are going to go through. Defining the process, mapping it and ensuring it is transparent with clear stages of implementation enables not only transparency but also allows opinions to be expressed in the right way and vitally at the right time. This removes the old group think mentality of everyone having an opinion and sharing it through informal networks and allows formal stepladders of information gathering to occur.

The gradual inclusion of people allows not only control of involvement but vitally it also allows leaders to bring in the right people at the right time. Bringing stakeholders in ensures leaders carry everyone with them and through stakeholder analysis of where people stand (background) and how influential they are time, effort and resources of leaders can be focused to where it is needed most to ensure the right environment for success is enabled.

The final piece of the jigsaw in creating the right environment is in making sure that the leaders are asking the right questions, the who, what, where, why, when and how, helps you identify the real underlying problem that you face. Asking the right questions at the outset not only builds confidence that the leaders know what they are doing for those around them but also that they are able to take into consideration the breadth of information they need to analyse. For that to happen, a positive environment is an essential ingredient if leaders are to get the support, resources and buy-in from other members of the leadership team, colleagues and stakeholders.

Leaders must lead that creation of a positive environment and the most effective way that leaders can do that is to have a clear goal to drive a positive environment.

Step 2: Generate Good Alternatives

For leaders to be effective in making decisions, they have to do the right research to generate the right alternatives. Researching options is an important skill for leaders. Too often poor strategic options are a result of leaders' just relying upon 'option A' not even considering alternatives and quite often ignoring counter-to-plan A information or discounting it as irrelevant. I am always amazed at how few options are considered in strategic planning, and not just by small organizations. Researching where an organization is going, looking to the future and over the horizon planning has to involve researching several options at the outset. It is therefore important not to start with a prejudice on the outcome. That way when researching where an organizing is going, looking at several viable alternatives is an essential first stage in providing the platform for success in decision-making in strategic planning.

Two other reasons why there are often a lack of alternative options considered is that strategic planning is not given enough time. The lack of time in relation to the end plan time is often short as is the quantity of time devoted to developing plans. The net result from both of these is that with limited time leadership is forced to reduce the scope of options that results in developing too few options and so narrowing the scope and therefore the range of options they need to consider early on as viable alternatives.

The second additional factor, which I see, is the lack of resources being provided at the outset of strategic planning. More resources are provided in researching the leaders next holiday than in developing their strategic plan. Sometimes the resources invested can look more like a part-time hobby by leadership teams rather than the most important and valuable activity they are about to undertake for their business. It is essential that resources from investing in market research to attending talks be properly resourced.

The more good options you consider, the more comprehensive your final decision will be. When you generate alternatives, leaders are forced to dig deeper, ask questions and look at the problem from different perspectives. The mindset **'what are the options out there,'** ensures leaders are more likely to make and effectively evaluate all the viable options and therefore make the best decision possible. Without reasonable alternatives, then an option of one does not leave a decision to make.

The classic tools I use in developing viable alternatives for decisions depend upon the nature of the business. In larger organizations, stakeholder mapping is essential, for buy-in but also for inclusion in generating ideas across the whole spectrum of skills and audiences.

Brainstorming is a popular idea generation method, engaging with generally smaller teams of people, who comfortably know each other to outline blue-sky thinking around where they are going and why. Using this type of format Edward De Bono's models such as 6 thinking hats can help to develop a 360-degree perspective of any ideas, by enabling any idea to be subject to scrutiny from six defined perspectives. Each 'hat' provides a view, which challenges the validity and voracity of the alternative. Similar ideas such as the reframing matrix assess an alternative by looking at it from the perspective of product, planning, potential and people. Models such as these also allow outsiders (experts) to join the discussion, or ask existing participants to adopt different functional perspectives to interrogate them for robustness.

Developing successful decision-making requires leadership to stand back from deciding which alternatives are preferred, leaders must remain objective.

This becomes a real challenge to the robustness of the assessment of alternatives if leaders **'decide on their favourite'** during the creation of alternatives, as it tends to favour one over others, resulting in more resources being allocated to 'plan A' while 'plan B' is not explored to the same extent. Alternative options need to be explored, resourced and thought through thoroughly to see the whole spectrum of alternatives not a narrow field around one leaders' preferred strategic option.

Step 3: Explore the Alternatives

Developing realistic alternatives, I always think that no more than 5 are possible to develop and for many 3 options with a couple of variations seems to be about the right number to reflect the variety of decision options you and your key stakeholders can buy into, particular when considering forward strategy.

With too many options it looks like a pick and mix of options, which while it has its attractions, you can appeal to everyone's taste, creates a cascade of problems in carrying people forward. I use an example of a shoe shop with business leaders with too many strategic options. While choice looks good in the window and gets people to come through the door it damages sales as people are spoilt for choice and instead of making a positive decision on anything they look, try and then walk away.

A good sports shoes shop invests in its staff developing their skills cutting down the options, just like folding a piece of paper, until you are left with a choice of 2. The secret is to ensure it is the customer who believes they have undertaken the cutting down (making the choice), and it is just the helpful staff assisting them to make the right choice. In reality it is the sole purpose of staff to lead the customer to the end result model A or B.

Step A - Are they male or female (direct them to the relevant section)?
Step B – What activity are they buying the shoes for? Direct them to the choices available.
Step C – What is their current shoes type, make model usage and likeability (preference) of brand?
Step D – Ask about shoe size and see if the popular brand model is available in that size.
Step E – Bring target brand model out and next price point model out in the right size.
Step F – If shoes sizes not available (shortage or not stocked minor size feet) then bring out next price point options to provide choice of 2.
Step G – Always give the customer 2 choices to try on and confirm good choice to decision making unit.

With any strategic decision-making process, having at least 2 options is vital, but for a more realistic assessment of where the market and your organization is heading 3 to 5 options are far more likely to occur if the horizon is more than a year ahead. When you're satisfied that you have a good selection of realistic alternatives, then you'll need to evaluate the feasibility, risks, and implications of each choice. Working out the impact of implications in making the decision to take one route compared to another.

In any business, public or community environment, the primary consideration in evaluation is that of risk in decision-making; there's usually some degree of uncertainty, which inevitably leads to risk. By evaluating the risk involved with various options, the leadership can determine whether the risk is manageable. Notice I use the term leadership here, not leader. When assessing risk, it is the leadership (formal and informal) who should be involved in assessing risk.

Assessing risk is all about risk analysis, a logical and inclusive objective study of the risk profile for assessing the nature and organizations approach and appetite for dealing with threats. Threats, the risks, come in 2 types the known threats, those which we can see and understand from knowledge, experience and understanding of the strategic options that the alternative proposes, and the unknown risks of working in any future market.

Risk analysis allows you to see and understand the risk factor and can be evaluated against probability of events occurring and appetite factors for risk, within the organization. Risk analysis allows the leadership to look at implications of undertaking a strategic decision and look at the potential consequences that arise from that decision. An impact analysis looks at how those consequences can be managed. For example how will the competitors react to your organization moving into a new market? By looking back at previous new entrants you can assess the known response options and which customers took which approach to minimize the impact of that type of change.

The second type of risk in strategic selection, which needs to be assessed, comes from the unknown risks associated with any strategic selection. What might happen to that market should a significant change happen to it suddenly? The way of dealing with this type of risk is to look at the resilience of your business modeling (the assumptions for growth, revenue, margin, customer acquisition etc.) you made and stress test it to see what the likely impact might be. This type of impact assessment is an important factor in assessing the unknown risk factors, which any forward strategic decision-making has to go under.

If you can see an emerging new market and forecast a reasonable percentage of the market share, or winning key customer segments, then it is likely that someone else has also seen that market and may launch at the same time as you intend to, targeting the same target audiences. When I look at business models and plans this second type of risk assessment is often the most telling in understanding the robustness and realistic assessment of the potential of any business plan. Leadership teams are often good at type 1 risk assessment and mitigation strategies; they have understood the functional risks well. But risk type 2 is the strategic risk assessment (the unknown risks) and they have assumed that all markets are stationary in the scenario planning. Essentially saying that while we are moving forward the competition will stay exactly where it is, or not move as fast.

By competition, I do not just mean the existing players within the market that the leadership team wishes to operate but also new entrants, possibly from other markets who might enter or substitute product options which can steal market share, but substituting need through alternative product or service offering. For example, the growth of mobile phone size is reducing usage of smaller tablets, something which is quite obvious to expect as they merge together in function and form, but it is has also driven up demand and usage for none tablet reading devices as many high value customer segments see the multi-functionality of the devices as distracting from the use of tablets as reading devices. This substitution factor has resulted in a shift within the market and has left the multi-functionality tablet players without access to key high value consumers as they have moved away to advanced but single use, reading products.

This example opens up the door to the next key element in exploring the alternatives you have created, that of validating which one is the preferred solution, which matches your strategic objectives. The business strategy that is most likely to work in the long term.

There are many models used to undertake feasibility assessment, from force-field analysis, assessing the pros and cons of each option through to cost-benefit analysis looking at the financial feasibility of an alternative. Typically leadership teams should look at both of these assessment methods. I am a huge advocate of starting with the end in mind in looking at feasibility. That means deciding on criteria from the objective (not subjective) point of view from the perspective of the end objective. If the objective is to enter a new market, I would start form the point of view of what does that market need and define the selection criteria for alternatives based around those factors. If it was internal stakeholder expectations of financial performance then I would recommend that their needs were the basis of where the assessment criteria should be drawn from.

Assessment needs to be undertaken by objective scrutiny and always focused on the vision, which the leadership team is committed to achieving.

Step 4: Choose the Best Alternative

Evaluation can be numeric, it can be qualitative and it can certainly be divisive, depending upon who is evaluating what and when. After evaluating competing alternatives the next step is to choose between them. The choice may be obvious, but often it is not. Split decisions, the unknown factor in forward strategy of looking beyond the horizon and scenario planning providing multiple options can all play into the hands of leaders differing in their opinions. Making a definitive choice between alternatives is about getting leadership teams and their influential stakeholders (shareholders, key customers, advisors etc.) to decide on a particular strategic option. To make a choice and not navel gaze, pondering and playing for time or some miracle cure to suddenly hit them.

The critical way to move the leadership team to make a decision is to use a decision matrix analysis tool. This type of assessment tool is an objective criteria agreed by everyone as the critical factors in making the assessment. These are weighted in response to the leadership teams (and other voices) concerns as to their relative importance and only factors that match absolute relevance are used as criteria.

Example of Decision Matrix Tool

Decision Matrix

	Criterion A	Criterion B	Criterion C	Criterion D	Total
Option 1					
Option 2					
Option 3					
	Criteria Weights				

It's invaluable because it helps you bring disparate factors into your decision-making process in a reliable and rigorous way. This model is highly useful when comparing multiple options with multiple criteria with different weightings. This models is very useful as it allows leaders an inclusive say in the outcome expressing their view on each alterative which when compiled produces an overall weighting factor, with the outcome score defining the preferred strategic route to take.

Other variations of decision tools such as paired comparison analysis are usually used when there are only two alternatives left. By using paired comparison analysis unlike factors are directly compared to define which ones carry the most weight. Decision trees on the other hand lay out the options and allow scenario planning of the likelihood of project success or failure into the decision making process.

Sometimes logical models do not carry the day and direct voting in a showdown environment, with a neutral 3rd party (experienced consultant acting as the honest, non-involved) host. This type of selection is most common when group decisions are required and the criteria are subjective and it's critical that the leaders gain consensus between themselves. Using multi-voting on priorities and end objectives is one effective tool, although leadership teams can spend more time laying out and redefining the rules than making progress. Other ways of deciding can include outsourcing the decision to an expert ('wise men') panel of neutral experts sometime chosen by Non-Executive Directors (NEDs) to make the decision. The Delphi Technique of a facilitator listening to reasoned argument within a timeframe can be also used; they act like a legal advocate and is usually reserved to very specialist areas where experts struggle to agree or vested interest personalities conflict.

The essential element of this phase in strategic decision-making is to ensure it has a proper, defined, agreed and time-bound timetable. Paralysis is the outcome of not making a decision. One technique I use with leadership teams here is the use of the Gap Analysis technique to assist (cattle-prod) leadership teams to make decisions.

The gap analysis technique looks at the impact of 'do nothing' on the business. By looking at the current critical performance criteria that are driving the need for the leadership assessing its strategy and where that is going over the next few years. You can show the leadership the impact of not making a decision. Plot against that the growth form option A and/or B and the gap in performance becomes visual and painful. Highlight the key numbers and hand it over to the leadership team to present as part of their decision-making and it is a powerful way to drive the need for making a decision, choosing the best alternate there is.

Linked to choosing the best alternative is to check your decision, not only with all those involved but also with what I call the sanity test. That is, to gain a perspective once the decision has been agreed from others outside the core inner circle, someone who is not affected by the sway of the leadership team but provides a fresh alternative. I do not mean someone with no knowledge of the subject, your 5-year-old child maybe the apple of your eye, but the future of your business may not be best decided by his or her view about your market over the next few years. An industry expert, a non-involved director, a loyal retired customer or retained technical expert may provide the sanity test which ensures you are not '**believing your own press**' which can happen as leadership teams become too involved in their strategy.

This step is part of the due diligence that involves quietly and methodically testing the assumptions and the decisions you've made against your own experience, and thoroughly reviewing and exploring any doubts you might have.
Coupled to this involves reviewing whether common decision-making problems like over-confidence, escalating commitment, may have undermined the decision-making process. Never underestimate the future; the market will change and if you are developing a new strategy it is most likely in response to changes already occurring. No man is an island and certainly no business is. How fast your competition can respond is likely to be a major limiting factor in how successful your strategy will be. That lead-time factor, the first mover advantage is always overstated in plans and the confidence it generates often fades faster than it should. So checking your assumptions is an important element in choosing the best option.
Step 5: Communicate Your Decision

You can't be a little bit pregnant. This is a phase I use with CEO's and leadership teams once they have made their decision. A conviction must exist in making the decision that only exists when tangibly the leadership team (note team, not leader) communicates the decision. It is important to explain it to those affected by it, and involved in implementing it. Talk about why the leadership chose the alternative you did. Put it in context with a simple and clear narrative explained by an executive summary, which all the leadership team can communicate effectively in number of ways to differing audiences. The more information you provide about risks and projected benefits, the more likely people are to support the decision.

I am a great believer in the power of the visual leadership in announcing strategic decisions. Not the email or report, but led form the top presentation, real or virtual where everyone can see the leadership say and commit to a decision and stand by their decision. Only once a decision is made does the real work of convincing people begin. The challenge is that for most a new strategy means little (or nothing) until it directly impacts upon people. Only when they have to change does it really matter.

Depending upon the size and nature of the business than can be tomorrow or in 3 years' time. So making the strategy live is about a great first and lasting impression. It has to be sold and sold by someone who owns the outcome and can communicate the WHY with passion. If people can see why they are being asked to do something different coupled with simple but immediate first steps then they are involved form day one and understand why they have to make that change.

Immediate inclusive and leadership led action is the most important step which the leadership team needs to make. Get people involved by focusing them to become involved from the start.

Talk is cheap; action is everything in leadership communication.

We have all been in meaningless and instantly forgettable meetings on a subject that has no direct correlation to what is on our agenda now. That is the reality that leaders have to face when announcing a decision on a strategy. Can they answer the 'so what' test in their communication with their strategy. Effective communication requires it to make an impact upon the audience so they do not just feel things will get better but they take ownership with passion for making it happen and can contribute to making it successful.

Simple inclusive first steps, from designing a process, or marketing collateral, or redefining their departments function are all ways which leaders can and do share the ownership for the strategy and gain not only involvement but also commitment to make it happen. This must also not only happen as a one-off but requires the leadership to continually drive the message home, with quick wins progress reports and enthusiasm backed up by the right level of resources to support progress.

Chapter 9   Why Do I Need a Strategic Plan?

The great advantage of a strategic plan is that it focuses everyone's attention around a core goal, a core vision of where you want to see your organization to be in the next 1, 3 or 5 years' time. That strategic plan enables people to understand how everyone is involved in making a change and where the organization's going as a big picture for the organization. That strategic plan, therefor carries and takes people forward to where you want them to be going and understanding how their role is today and what it needs to look like tomorrow in achieving the big picture for the organization.

Write it down

Writing down your strategic plan is vital because firstly it encourages people to focus on what they are doing and why, it asks the questions: 'why are we undertaking this planning process and what is our end goal in achieving things?' It gives a clear direction to what the business is doing and it gains commitment from everyone involved in the planning process - one of the key outcomes of why you develop and write down a plan. It also enables you to think, review, plan and interrogate your actions as to what you are actually intending to achieve. That questioning ability is a really important focus of what writing down a plan is all about. The next key thing it does is deliver a commitment to the plan. It actually puts it on paper and stops it just being an idea in your head. Coupled with that is that you gain buy in from people and one of the problems people have with any planning process or making any change is gaining buy in from those not directly involved. So any opportunity to write things down is a chance to actually get people bought into the process and to get them to see the future and be part of it and commit to the final part which is action planning. What changes are going to happen and when, where and why in terms of the undertaking of the planning process? So actually the planning process itself is of vital importance, the plan is merely the tangible outcome that supports and then drives the next stage of what you are trying to achieve.

Chapter 10   The Elements of Successful Strategy

The phrase strategy is one of the most overused phrases in business today; every leader uses the word to define everything they are doing with their business. It is used to describe not only real strategic planning outcomes but also tactical activities and other business activities, including good luck and competitor misfortune. Strategy is not a plan in someone's head, an idea or concept, it has to be a tangible, living, breathing entity within the business. Something, which is not only seen (tangible) to exist, but which people work towards (living) and which people talk about (breathing). The business strategy should be lived by those whose role it is to deliver it and able to be understood at headline level by everyone.

A business strategy must live beyond a department or a trading season, if not then it is a tactic, a short-term initiative. Tactics are the opportunities, which a leader takes either within their department or as a business to take advantage of an immediate opportunity. For example if a competitor offers a price reduction to drive up their sales and you match it to maintain your market share. This does not make you a price cutter, which is a strategy; it is a tactical decision to retain your market position. Should you decide to keep discounting price to win market share for the long term, by cutting all costs within the business, outsourcing high cost essential items such as manufacturing, or call centre activity, remove all layers of unneeded value within the marketing and operations which does not fit with the low cost model, then strategically you would be a low cost supplier.

Strategy is a therefore a more than just taking advantage of an opportunity it is:

"an integrated set of choices that uniquely positions the firm in its industry, so as to create sustainable advantage and superior value relative to the competition." Lafley and Martin

There are many tools used in developing strategy, covering every aspect of strategy development. We have so many tools, such as PESTLE, five-forces analysis, core competencies, hyper-competition, the resource-based tools, (just to mention a few) all providing a view of some aspect of the future. The problem, which I come across fairly commonly, is for the strategist to take a narrow view of research, relying upon the one tool they like, or have commissioned from a specialist consultancy firm to undertake one piece of research, from which they draw the conclusions they want to see.

This classic overreliance upon one tool, or 'narrow thinking' not only provides a poor insight into strategic options but is often engineered towards a preconceived outcome which the research was commissioned to confirm. Even a well-considered aspirational strategy itself is vital for leadership to succeed, and likewise without great leadership even the best strategy will not succeed.

"Strategy is not primarily about planning. It is about intentional, informed, integrated proactive decision-making".

I have recently been working with a global FMCG company on developing their business strategy, as part of my research prior to starting work with them, they proudly supplied me with a copy of a huge report (200 pages) into their market from a highly regarded global consultancy brand, for which they had paid a considerable sum of money, but which told them that they were operating in a complex market. It provided lots of data, but limited information from which intelligence could be drawn.

Many strategists who are drawn to Porter's five-forces analysis tend to think of strategy as a matter of selecting industries and segments within them.

This type of problem called 'strategic fragmentation' is accelerating as narrowly specialized consultants have started plying their single tools in the name of strategy. The artificial evolution of these single tools to stretch them to cover every aspect of strategy, extrapolates data form one area to infer outcomes elsewhere, reduces its credibility and often overstates the importance of one data source. This double risk, of data stretch and double valuing data devalues through one single tool undermines the pure nature of the original tool and reduces trust in the strategic process.

"Using only one strategic tool to define an organization strategy is like playing golf with only one club."

If you are going to develop your business successfully, whether as a new start-up with a blank piece of paper or take a well-established company forward then you need to focus on the complete strategic picture, as outlined below by Hambrick and Fredrickson model, the whole process not just the piece(s) the leadership likes, or wants to see.

A strategy consists of an integrated set of choices, but it isn't a catchall for every important choice an executive faces. As Hambrick and Fredrickson's model below demonstrates the company's mission and objectives, for example, stand apart from, but are inextricably linked to the strategy. While the two are directly linked, you can't achieve the objectives without the strategy, it is useful to be able to separately identify each of the component elements, to enable different audiences (stakeholders) to engage and participate in the process.

Similarly, because strategy addresses how the business intends to engage its environment, choices about internal organizational arrangements are not an integral part of strategy. By moving the implementation of organizational arrangements out from the strategy, that enables the strategy to be kept clean, clear and central to the organization's future.

So leaders when developing their strategy should not write documents on compensation policies, information systems, or training programs as being strategy. While these are critically important elements of implementation but by not throwing everything into the strategy bucket, you make the strategy a robust and coherent headline document, which reinforces the consistency among the elements of the strategy itself.

The Elements of Strategy

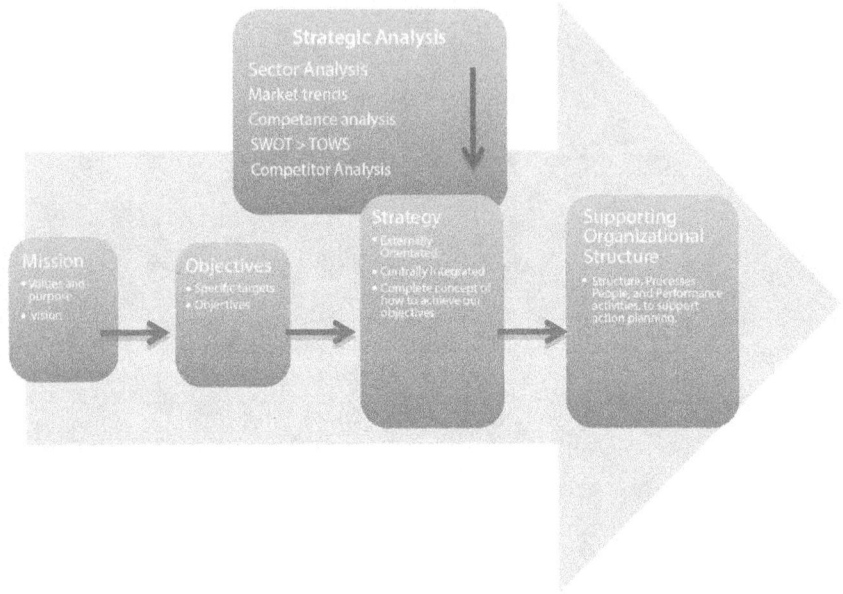

(after Hambrick and Fredrickson)

The Elements of Strategy

If a business must have a strategy, then the strategy must necessarily have parts. A strategy has five elements, providing answers to five questions:

- Markets: where will we be operating?
- Routes to market: how will we get there?
- Differentiators: how will we win in the market place?
- Financial Model: how does the model stack-up, the Return-On-Investment (ROI)?
- Action planning: what are the key steps and milestones of achievement towards our goals?

These five main elements must be answered for any strategy to be successful. The importance of being able to provide coherent answers to those 5 key questions is fundamental for leaders to carry their organization forward. The key inputs to any strategy is the strategic analysis, which informs all the elements of the strategy. The inputs from strategic analysis therefore support the outcomes, providing leaders with the credibility of their decision-making.

When you look at the above model, the reality is that if the business strategy is to be successful then the key decisions about Markets, Routes to market, Differentiation and Action planning must all tie in and back with the Financial Model. If it does not add up then it is not thought out effectively enough.

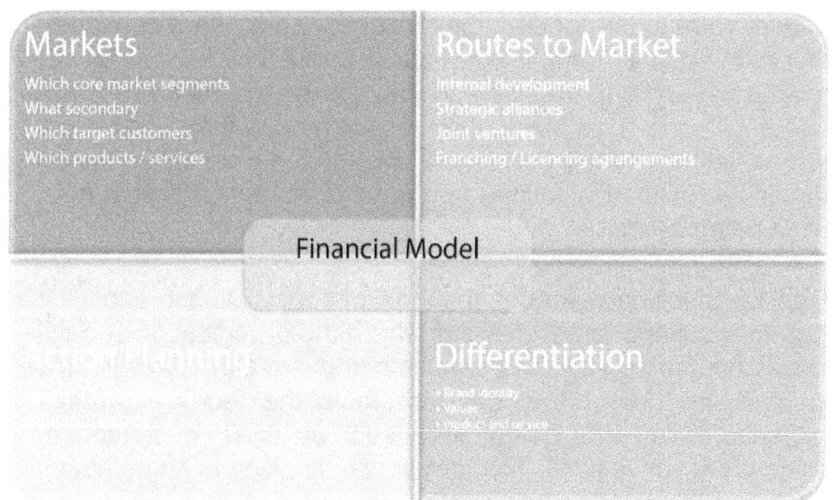

Markets

The most fundamental choices leaders make are those of where, or in what markets the business will be active. Many leaders use phrases such as "we will be the leader in XYZ technology" this creates a problem of generality; it is vague and more aspirational than market specific. It is important to be as specific as possible about the product categories, market segments, geographic areas, and core technologies, as well as the value-adding stages (e.g. sourcing, product design, manufacturing, selling, and reselling)

When I work with leadership teams I always challenge generalities of market leadership. What does that mean, which market, which products, which subsectors of the market. When leaders talk about a market, be like a sniper not a blunderbuss user. Too many leaders want to be general, they want to operate and be players in every market they can. This is usually caused by the fear of not covering everything they can do. Being a jack-of-all-trades and a master of none. This pull to the masses means that many good companies are poorly positioned towards the markets where they should be focused to trying to be generalists operating but not succeeding in any.

The fear of losing overrides the logic of specialising in and therefore owning target markets where the organization should focus and specialise.   The causes of this are either lazy thinking, (not thinking through the repercussions of the decision), or the influence of powerful stakeholders such as legacy customers or dumb money investors. The former lazy thinking is something, which is as frustrating as it is a self-limiting decision, which many leaders regret. The root cause of this type of poor decision making is not thinking through the long-term impact of being too general in any market, trying to keep every market and every customer means that an organization is overstretched and under resourced resulting in it losing its competitive advantage over time.

These uniformed voices often drive leaders not to be precise as to which markets they wish to target. Like a good sniper, selecting your target is about focusing on the precise growth market you want to target.

The challenge for market selection is to be as specific as possible. In choosing markets it is about defining each and by priority within market selection. Some market segments, for instance, might be identified as centrally important, with key target customers by name or type, while others are deemed secondary or tertiary. A strategy might reasonably be centred on one product category, such as flagship launching to generate the right market entry strategy to a new market, while to resource that investment elsewhere in established markets may have to be delayed to a later date.

Routes To Market

While market identification is central to any business strategy, being able to get to those markets is vital. Are they accessible and in what is the best way to access those markets and to operate within them? Specifically, the means for attaining the needed presence in a particular product category, market segment, geographic area, or value-creation stage should be the result of deliberate strategic decision. If the leadership decides to expand into new markets, how is it going to accomplish that? Organic growth is slow and expensive to redeploy but other routes to market, such as joint ventures, using agencies, franchising, licencing, acquisitions or other vehicles could achieve that quicker and offer a better means for achieving the leaders key goals.

Routes to market really matter, if you cannot get to a market, then your strategy will never succeed.

Route-to-market selection is not part of the implementation phase, a secondary consideration, it is central to the reality of a leaders' plan. Without it there is no credible plan. If you can't get to market, then your strategy will never succeed. Failure to explicitly consider and articulate the intended routes to market will result in entry being either significantly delayed or not achievable.

There are steep learning curves associated with the use of alternative expansion modes. How an organization learns to expand, either into new territories locally or through international expansion can be a major competitive advantage. Often in high value markets being able to define coherent access to them geographically can provide a very profitable and robust expansion strategy.

Differentiation

How an organization wins in any market, how it will get customers to come its way is its winning strategy. In a competitive world, winning is the result of sustainable differentiation within its industry sector. Global brands use their brand identity to sustain differentiation, but this can be easily diluted (or destroyed) by localisation of brands to different markets or by multiple sub brands, which can crowd out brand identity.

Every brand, no matter how big or small must differentiate itself to its target audience.

Creating a sustainable and compelling marketplace advantage does not necessarily mean that the company has to be at the extreme on one differentiating dimension, or rely upon its marketing strategy to define the brand strategy. Some of the best strategies use simple combination of differentiators, such as how the brand does business or where it does business, which can be created by the brand strategy. For example being first into a new market is often a clear differentiator, from credit cards that are usable in more places around the world than any other, to the ubiquity of brands such as Coca Cola (there is only one market (2015) where you cannot buy Coca Cola and that is North Korea). This type of strategy enables brands to develop their strategy through global differentiation rather than fighting each market with different differentiation strategies.

Differentiation must therefore be central to the strategy selection process and not handed over to the marketing strategy, further down the business planning process. Differentiation should be one of the five central pillars of strategy selection. How you enter a market and how you differentiate within your markets matters. Look at Ben and Jerry's Ice Cream, which up against established brands such as Haagen-Dazs, chose to enter markets through quirky products and marketing targeting its precise audience in every market. Another brand Red Bull chose its strategy to be associated with unusual high adrenaline sports as a strategy, which has enabled the brand to clearly differentiate itself from any other in its industry and sustain that differentiation globally.

Action planning

The importance of successful action planning is the move from theory to reality. Without the ability to turn ideas into action, the strategy is just a dream. Understanding what needs to happen and when is a fundamental part of the leadership team's role in creating a successful strategy. It is the action planning that determines the resource requirements of the strategy selection, which in turn defines the economic modelling of the strategy.

Action panning is about understanding the staging of events that will have to happen to achieve what in which order. For action planning to be successful then it is essential that the leadership team start with the end in mind. To achieve our end objective any strategy must communicate 'what will it look like?' Just as with a world-class sports person, visualising winning is the end step from which all others begin. At school the number of times I had to practice scoring a try in rugby union so that it became second nature to me, is as important as making my first tackle. In just the same way the All Blacks practice the Hakka, their ritual challenge before each game to the competition, not just so it intimidates the competition but so it becomes part of the routine for winning, something they do quite well.

Action planning is not only a reality check or the viability of any business strategy, but also a resource gap definer. What do we have and what do we need to deliver our chosen strategy. What new is needed is usually fairly obvious at this stage, people and investment always top the list for virtually every company, but one item which leaders shy away from is change. Change starting with them. If there organization is to compete what do they have to do differently. Telling others is easy, looking at the leadership to see what skills they have, they need and must do differently is more often than not missed of the initial actions of the leadership team's action plan, and yet without the leaders doing what is needed nothing will change.

Action planning also provides a timeframe for implementation. It needs to reflect seasonal factors within markets, development time for new products and services and above all the time it takes to find, recruit and train people prior to them developing results. I always love seeing an implementation plan where day one a new person with the right skills will appear (be poached or lifted) and then one day they will deliver amazing results. Finding people takes months, start at 3 and work forwards from there. Once found they have to be moved across, that will take time, and they will have to adjust and learn how the company works, forge new relationships and fit in with the buying cycle. Realistically the timescale before any results start to appear (and return-on-investment) may take up to a year depending upon circumstances.

Another essential factor is the pursuit of early or quick wins. Strategic thinking always includes quick wins to offset investment and timeframes. They are dropped in to fill the hole in expectations of stakeholder returns. Quick wins, the short term successes that occur because you launch a new strategy are not only improvements to the economic model but also morale boosters, when a large unexpected customer suddenly buys form you, or a competitor's new product fails to arrive on time and a target customer gives you that fantastic call.

I remember working at Berghaus in the late 1980's and we had low market penetration of high quality retailers in London, when

Lillywhites (at the time the benchmark of retailing excellence in central London, knocked through a wall to find the boarded up ballroom of what had been a hotel, unused since the beginning of world-war2 when a bomb had gone through and it had been abandoned. The call from the head buyer, can you help fill 5,000 square feet with your own shop, solved the problem in an instant. I have never seen a leadership team move so fast to get up to London, with YES we can, a quick win which resolved the issue overnight. It was a genuine quick win which delivered real results, which accelerated our penetration strategy of high value markets, but it was only a quick win, not the strategy itself.

Quick wins matter, but often they are small in terms of overall impact and more often than not as Woody Allen is quoted as saying: "80% of success is turning up" Simply being in the market will generate success, which with a strategy in place will support sustained success.

Financial Model

At the heart of a business strategy must be a clear idea of how strategy will deliver improved financial performance. Unless there is a compelling basis for the strategy to be adopted financially it won't be. Improved turnover used to be the most important criteria but in today's rapidly changing globally open market, margin matters more than ever and that means winning and retaining the right type of customer. That's where strategies add-up and becoming compelling.

Will the target customers pay more and if so why and how much? Will the plan be economically viable under stress testing to see what happens if revenues are not as good, the competition quicker to respond or the pace of introduction slower and more costly?

Any strategy has to make sense financially and there has to be a compelling basis for it.

The most successful strategies have a central economic logic, which has driven their creation and which serves as the fulcrum for profit creation. In some cases, the economic key may be to obtain premium prices by offering customers a difficult-to-match product. Launching flagship products and services with defensible premium priced attributes is at the heart of brand leaders in any market. It is the strategy for premium products and services in every consumer market that longevity is a central pillar of the purchase package.

A classic alternative premium strategy used in high performance products from Gillette razors to Nespresso coffee is to offer relatively low cost access to the product but high cost disposable items that only work with the product. So Gillette razors are affordable in every market, but the unique blades are a high premium, the unique coffee capsules that fit the Nespresso machine are described as the most expensive coffee in the world. This is just one alternative that makes the economic model work for these brands. Just like car servicing at dealers, brand entry has been reduced to maximise the market opportunity but the relative cost of use is high.

Strategic Comprehensiveness

As can be seen from the above, strategy needs to encompass all five elements, markets, routes, differentiation, action planning and financial modelling for it to be successful. All five are essential and therefore equally important and therefore require the same investment of time and skills to ensure strategic success. I am always surprised how many strategic plans over emphasize one or two of the elements without giving any consideration to the others. Yet to develop a strategy without attention to all five leaves critical omissions. No plan survives first contact with the enemy, but without all 5 elements thought through, no plan should ever be approved.

Any strategic plan must be rounded, coherent and logical if it is to be a solid platform from which any organization is able to believe in.

All the elements of a strategy must inter-relate and they must align with and support each other. Each of the four ground work pillars, markets, routes to market, differentiators and action planning must all interlink and support the economic model. Most leaders like certain parts of these pillars. The accountants love the financial model and often miss out the robustness of the assumptions it is built upon. Sales directors like markets, but not the routes to market. Marketers love differentiation, they see it as marketing but it is not, it is the essence of the brand strategy elevated to the brand strategy, the differentiation in the market, not the marketing strategy, which is a separate divisional activity. The generalist director, the corporate body often focuses on the outputs not the inputs that are required to inform the strategy itself.

These central input elements are the high level outputs from strategic planning from which operational detail is developed. It is at this high level stage which leadership teams need to think through and devise their strategy. Undertaking all 5 elements provides robustness and a sanity test as to the strategic credibility of any strategic plan.

It is only after the complete specification of all five strategic elements that the leadership is in the best position to turn to the other supporting activities, the functional and operational plans, from operating programs and processes which underpin and enable the action plan to deliver the strategy.

Strategy is worthwhile because many leaders have lost track of what it means to engage in the art of strategy. The recent catchall fragmentation of the strategy concept, the most abused term in business today, often means in just having an idea, with little or no integrity behind it. This type of visionary strategy has to be sold, but does not stand up to scrutiny and often fails because of the lack of research. Visionary strategies rely upon super salesmen whose passion drives the strategy forward. Super salesmen have to make promises and use their personality to make the strategy live. The lack of robust data, information and intelligence often means that many strategies are generic in nature, 'to be number 1' or 'the Apple of our industry'.

The dumbing down of strategy to be just a generic statement without the robust integrity means that strategy does not get the resources in time, people and skilled outside support. A successful business needs not just a strategy, but also a sound strategy. Some strategies are clearly far better than others. There are a number of quality strategic-analysis tools that research and inform business strategy. Such tools as industry analysis, technology cycles, value chains and core competencies among others, are very helpful for improving the robustness of strategies.

Chapter 11   Strategic Tools External Analysis

Central to any leader's thoughts on strategy is to focus on the key drivers of change within their market. The focus of many leaders is on what is happening within their market, but not on understand the key drivers of change. If leaders focus on the impact of change they are likely to be responding to changes, and therefore reactive in their thinking, responding to changes once they have occurred.

This causes several problems. Firstly, being reactive makes the organization, and your leadership slow to respond. Brand leaders within any field, the early adopters will already have seen these changes and responded to them reducing your value to them and reducing your ability to work with them, you have sacrificed the market leading position to someone else. Secondly, responding to change once the event has happened, while it is always safer to be second in a market rather than first, you often face higher costs in having to respond quicker, with fewer options as market positions, as product and service options have already been taken, and face the real challenge of how to respond in accordance within your business model.

Strategic leadership is therefore not about seeing what has happened and responding to it as best you can, it is seeing what is about to happen because you are looking at the root causes, the drivers of change and then can understand not only the impact but all the likely consequences that change may lead to.

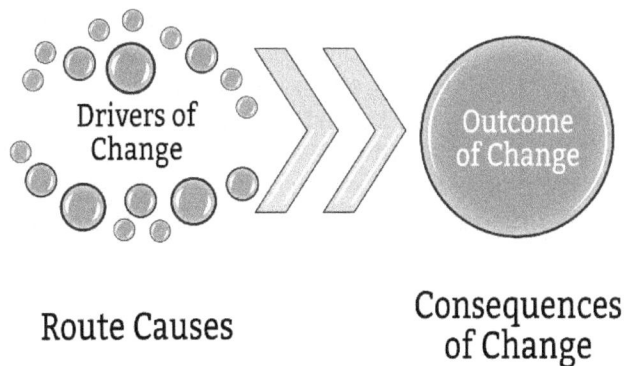

Route Causes   Consequences
                             of Change

This proactive mental approach is fundamental to strategic leadership. It is the type of thinking which leaders do when looking to enter a new market but once they are established within a sector it is a mental process that can become forgotten and leaders rely upon industry knowledge, customer insights and shear instinct. These are all skills that focus on responding to emerging change rather than understanding the drivers of it. The key tool in being proactive rather than reactive in understanding the drivers of your market is called PESTLE. The PESTLE analysis should be used to provide a context for the organization's / individual's role in relation to the external environment.

PESTLE as an acronym stands for Political, Economic, Social, Technological, Legal and Environmental factors. These key factors, the driver elements of change are the areas in which the strategic leader should investigate to look for drivers. Now there are many versions of PESTLE, depending on which elements are relevant to a market or industry, so it can also be referred to as STEP, STEEP, PESTEL, PESTLE or LEPEST. In certain markets it has also been further extended to STEEPLE and STEEPLED, including education and demographics. Your choice is to identify which driver elements are relevant to your sector. To me when working with any industry the original STEP (Social, Technological, Economic and Political) are the core ones, but I struggle to see any business sector when Environmental and Legal drivers should not be considered. I therefore always focus on PESTLE, but education and demographic are important factors in certain sectors, where global markets are being considered for example, or in directly affected industries such as educational, and that is where STEEPLE becomes an effective analysis of external drivers of your market. For example, I recently undertook a STEEPLE analysis for a software IT company operating in the schools educational market, where both demographics and education were fundamental drivers of change and opportunity identification to their industry.

The identification of drivers within these factors must be assessed either as macro (e.g. World-, EU- or UK-wide) or micro (e.g. institutional or individual) level.

The scope and scale of the leaders' research must be focused around investigating the factors for the drivers of change within each category in descending order:

1. What is happening within each category, which is driving change?
2. Which are likely to be most important in a few years?
3. What are the impacts of any change upon your market?

Political: What are the key political drivers of relevance?
Worldwide, Regional and Government directives: funding at local level (council policies), national and local organizations' requirements, and institutional policy.
Governments drive change through policy and investment, both direct as a buyer and as creators of market changes.

Economic: What are the important economic factors?
Where is the economy growing: globally, regionally, locally, industry and subsector specific: where in your sector growth coming from. Where growth is coming from is an important attribute, and identifying the economic long-term trend within a sector or subsector is important to identify future trends.

Social: What are the main societal and cultural aspects?
Societal attitude changes are vital to identify, particularly in relation to new opportunities. How is society changing its attitudes to a subject, from online shopping to marriage are drivers of change, and by country and national demographics matter. Also general lifestyle changes, changes in populations, distributions and demographics and the impact of different mixes of cultures all matter in understanding the drivers of change.

Technological: What are current technology requirements, changes and innovations?
What are the major current and emerging technologies of relevance within your industry sector? What is driving change and

what will the impacts of those changes look like to customers within your market? How customers engage and use technology is a major driver of opportunity within markets.

Legal: Current and impending legislation affecting your market. New and proposed legislation creates major changes in every industry; so knowing what legislation is likely to occur is an important external market analysis to undertake.
International, regional and national proposed and passed legislation are important drivers of change, including trading block changes.

Environmental: What are the environmental considerations, globally, regionally and nationally which affect your market? The environment since the late 1980's has become an important driver of change and in consumer and business behaviour.

The PESTLE analysis typically is most effective if it is reduced to an extendable table, which enables it to be referenced. There are endless variations of the table below, with weighting and rating of impacts, qualifying factors etc., but the fundamental point is that the leadership has a clear picture of the driving factors of their market.

FACTOR	DRIVER of CHANGE	CHANGE to MARKET	IMPACT of CHANGE	LIKELIHOOD of HAPPENING	OPPORTUNITY
Political					
Economic					
Social					
Technology					
Legal					
Environmental					

This PESTLE analysis is the primary tool for understanding the drivers of change within the market sector you are planning to operate within. The factors you identify inform the situation analysis or SWOT analysis, by identifying the opportunities and threats for your strategic planning.

Chapter 12   5 Forces

We have looked at the external drivers of any market, the PESTLE analysis. The PESTLE tells the leadership team what is driving its market externally. This external set of 'hidden forces', often not immediately seen by those inside a market, which drive it as the unseen hand of any market can take time to have a direct impact upon any market.

Contrary to those there are 'seen forces' from within any market, direct drivers of change, often shorter term, more visual, and more direct influences on any market. These internal market forces drive markets season to season and can be analyzed.

Known by any professional marketer as Kotler's 5 Forces analysis, this powerful tool is a vitally important analysis to undertake of any market. Markets are evolving, changing all the time. There is no status quo in any market, just a picture of any market at any time. Depending upon the market its rate of change will vary, external drivers often cause huge jumps, technology or social changes rapidly create revolutionary change, while economic and political changes make (usually) slower changes.

Markets are dynamic, self-organized and organically evolving; business like nature abhors a vacuum.

What drives change within markets are usually more immediate; annual, seasonal, or even quicker. These changes are part of the market dynamic within which every business operates and are the most immediate factors or drivers of change. The drivers Kotler organized into 5 forces which impact upon any and every market.

The forces reflect the powers that can impact upon every market. Each force has different values in different markets and within markets they differ depending upon where in any market you are at any time. The 5 forces look at the impact of each of the forces on any market and by definition upon any company operating within that market.

The 5 Forces Summary

Measuring the 5 forces defines your internal market structure

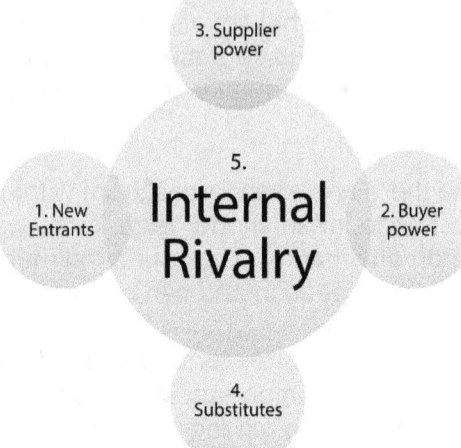

The 5 Forces

1. **New Entrants**
   The first and primary impact on any market is the arrival of
   new entrants. The impact of new entrants into any market
   is the single biggest potential threat to any market. The
   growth of supermarkets in developed markets around the
   world is because they wait until a market sector is
   developed by others and becomes sizable and therefore
   profitable enough for a low cost, efficient supplier with an
   infrastructure able to move volume and terms of trading
   which financially enable them to buy, sell and rebuy
   several times over before having to pay for the initial stock.
   Therefore all they had to do was to put on price incentives
   and a good layout to take market share from price-
   sensitive shoppers. This had enabled supermarkets to
   become a new entrant into markets as diverse as camping,
   home goods, pharmaceuticals, not to mention alcohol.

   Potential new threats to any market need to be assessed
   as to their likely impact. Who would a new entrant target
   and in what way? What defensive strategies can a

company take to defend against new entrants? Well established major market players can develop defensive strategies prevent or minimize the opportunity of new entrants. Often by working with mid-market players' major brands can put in place defensive strategies to prevent identified new entrants accessing the market. Other strategic options include planning for that entrant to come into the market by planning around the loss of certain market customers.

2. Buyer Power

The second most important factor in driving an internal market is the bargaining power of buyers within any market. If they are strong then they determine the nature and profitability of the companies within that market. Buyer power is always about driving prices down within any market, devaluing the market value and driving structural change within any market.

The result of high buyer power is that a market moves from value added product focus (depending upon the market, it could be technology, products or services), to focusing on price led factors. How buyers negotiate terms and conditions of payment and how they differentiate brands and the impact cost of switching brands to the companies they represent. High buyer power often leads to the growth of outsourcing rather than in-house ownership. The focus on logistics and other Value chain areas away from research and development of product becomes more significant.

Buyers are powerful because they make markets work, particularly in established markets. How the buying process works is therefore central to the operation of any developing or mature market. What they buy and when they buy is a key factor in the success of every market. The customer is king, is a phrase which everyone in business is very familiar. The structure of any free market is led by the bargaining power of the buyers, the budget holders, who make or break any market.

The leadership needs to understand the nature of the buyer structure within their market (or target market if looking to enter a new market). How much power do the buyers have and where does that real power lie within the buying structure? Who are the early adopters (market makers), compared to the market followers, the majority of buyer cash value.

3. **Supplier Power**
   The third element to consider is the power of the suppliers, those who supply the market. Suppliers to a market are always looking to drive prices up, to create value, which supports the supply chain to any market. Suppliers to any market are at the most important and most powerful early on in any markets creation. As new markets emerge suppliers secure their positioning through agreements such as preferred supplier, or through unique technology they provide, think Intel chips in computers. Powerful suppliers are vital for high value markets, where developing new technology, products or services drive the establishment or continued development of a market. Suppliers are often market makers, driving the leading edge of new markets. The ability for suppliers to drive up prices is ultimately controlled by how many suppliers there are and the structure of the market.

   The fewer the supplier choices the market has, the more they need the suppliers' assistance, and subsequently the more powerful the suppliers are. In many markets vertical integration, such as Sony's vertical market for films, they control not only the retailing and replaying of them, but also the writing, manufacture and distribution of films through their own film studio.

4. **Substitutes**
   The fourth force, the hidden force is the threat of

Substitution. This force is one of the subtle but important forces, particularly in consumer powerful markets, markets where the customer has choices. Substitution is the opportunity for the customer to solve the problem using alternative means. Substitution is often the way a new process, technique or technology gets into a market, but it is also a reason why customers can opt out of your market into another. Rather than reading physical newspapers, customers can read online news feeds to gain the same experience. This type of substitution can be both forward substitutions, new ways of doing something from outside your market (often technology led), or direct substitution by using alternative methods to solve what your market place provides.

Being able to substitute a major challenge which If it is easy and viable, and then this weakens the power of any market.

5. **Internal Rivalry**
   The final and most powerful internal force inside every market, and therefore the most important to measure, is the internal rivalry within any market. The number, competitive structure and capability of competitors to actively compete with each other is the most obvious sign of a markets virility. If a market has many competitors, and they offer equally attractive products and services, then competitive rivalry will be slight, as they will have little power in the situation, because suppliers and buyers will have a number of alternative options to take.
   On the other hand, if there are few dominant players then they will use their tremendous strength to outcompete each other and limit the attractiveness to new entrants.

   Competitive rivalry is also not universal within an industry, so when you measure it remember to look for where it exists, and where it does not. Rivalry always exits at the top of any market, the fight for number one is typically fierce, and not just in the private sector, many public institutions compete to be number one, from education to government departments. Niche points in any market also drive rivalry, subset markets with a market, or certain positions such as premium positions with certain customers.

Measuring the 5 Forces

The relative power of each factor is important and can be measured by scoring each of the forces within your market. The simplest technique is to identify the precise power and impact of each of the 5 Forces within your market (or target market). Weighting and rating them and identifying key defining factors that determine and control your market, summarized below.

5 Forces Model Benefits Summary

1. Strategic Use:
    Switching costs
    Access to distribution
    Economies of scale

2. Strategic Use:
    Buyer Selection
    Switching Costs
    Differentiation

3. Supplier power

5. **Internal Rivalry**

1. New Entrants

2. Buyer power

4. Substitutes

3. Strategic Use:
    Selection of Supplier
    Upward price driver
    Investment driven change

5. Strategic Use:
    Differentiation
    Market Access Control
    Cost-Effectiveness

4. Strategic Use:
    Redefinition of market
    Improved pricing
    Technology improvement

Chapter 13   Core Competence Model

Business is about winning; it is only about winning. But what makes a business win within its market? In running any business or organization the leadership team needs to know what its business is good at and how to use those skills to their advantage. That means identifying a company's core competencies, what it is good at and why, its strengths and in doing so things which it is not good at (its weaknesses).

It is not just the simple efficient v effectiveness debate, but it is a good place to start. The leadership of any company or organization must understand its core strengths within its market if it is to leverage them successfully to gain advantage within that market. Efficiency, is doing things right, while effectiveness is doing the right things. Success in business is combining the two.

McKinsey S7 Model

The McKinsey model is a very useful template from which to look at any organization holistically rather than by department. It identifies not only the hard factors of any company the hard S factors (in blue) below, of strategy, structure and systems, but also the soft S factors, (in red) as well as the shared values which connects all the S elements together.

The S 7 Model.

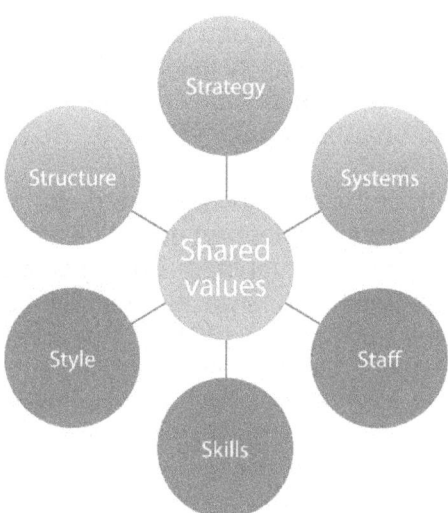

Assessing a company for its strengths (and weaknesses) using this S7 process is more objective and allows the leadership team to use both efficiency measures and effectiveness measures to assess their strengths (and weaknesses).

Efficiency

The efficiency assessment of doing things right, looks at how the organization operates as a cost effective deliverer. Led by repetition or skill set advantages, but also in developing and delivering processes and procedures as people personal skills, which make the business efficient in its activity within its market.

Efficiency is often a numeric measure of specific strengths. Efficiency strengths are easiest to identify and can be used by leadership teams to benchmark their business compared to competitors.

Efficiency is a competitive advantage if recognized and used to win business through leverage of that efficiency in the market. Coca-Cola measures its competitive advantage as an efficient brand, 1.9 billion servings per day, 250 bottling partners as the world's largest beverage company. Efficiency such as outsourcing, removing comparative high cost activities to parties who can undertake any activity at a lower total cost than the business undertaking that activity itself. Other outsourcing can be undertaken not just to make cost savings but also to create strategic supply or channel relationships.

Efficiency throughout the supply chain is a major advantage, which organizations from supermarkets (think Aldi in retailing) utilize to gain competitive advantage. Driving cost out of logistics in Western Europe has led to large international businesses being able to outcompete national companies. The creation of in-house and outsourced logistics is about creating efficiency through adapting manufacturing models such as lean manufacturing and Just in Time supply to drive efficiency by removing non value-added activities.

Efficiency is commonly uses by accountants (finance) to drive change, to ask why are we spending this amount in this area? This type of questioning by leaders is always valuable, but should not be undertaken on its own. While it is an excellent way to review cost structures and redefine the business model and is used to create lean cost effective businesses, it can result in an over focus on cost cutting rather than opportunity maximization.

Any business, which just cuts costs, is unlikely to deliver growth over the long term. Cutting costs is a very short benefit in any business. While it is necessary to regularly undertake, it does not deliver shareholder value unless that saving is re-invested in areas of growth. To succeed every business needs to look at where it is effective within its market. Where it delivers what customers need even if they do not know that they need it. For example retail buyers, if asked, will always tell you that price is THE important consideration when making a purchase consideration, but in fact to buyers in making a profitable purchase, the rate of sale and achieved margin, are the most important real determinants in bottom-line profitability.

Effectiveness

While efficiency, doing the things right, is always an important element is assessing strengths, more importantly to leadership is how effective it is as an organization. Effectiveness, doing the right things, are measures of strengths as outcomes. Being effective is not the opposite of being efficient, it is the important other half which not only compliments but often identifies vital and more important strengths for growth.

What is effectiveness inside a business and why does it matter in assessing strengths? Because, in essence what any business does effectively are the key strengths of any business. Being effective at any aspects of business is what gives any organization its key strengths. Effectiveness is the intangible value a business has, which is often seen as emotional strengths an organization has, while efficiency is often seen as numeric strengths.

For example, efficiency may be demonstrated by numeric facts, such as opening and closing ratios, or stock turn ratios or benchmark comparisons. Alternatively effectiveness is a useful measure of perceptions around a company. How well a company can do things is how effective it is, from measures of innovation to the strengths of relationships with customers, being effective is an essential measure of the soft measures of strengths.

Models such as Porters value chain is an excellent way of assessing where a business adds value and where by definition any business (or organization) does not add real value to customers.

Porter's Value Chain

Support activities	Organization
	Human Resources
	Technology
	Purchasing

Primary activities	Inbound Logistics	Operations	Outbound Logistics	Marketing and Sales	Service
	Materials handling Delivery	Manufacturing Assembly	Order processing Shipping	Product Pricing Promotion Place	Customer service Repair

Michael Porter

The great advantage of strategic business models such as the value chain is that they allow leaders to review their existing operation, or if starting from new plan out a model which enables them to focus on value added rather than classic benchmarking planning where leadership teams merely replicate existing competitors without thinking through where the real value is to their customers. Examples such as in countries like India who instead of covering their huge country in copper wires to provide a national telephone service just put up relatively cheap mobile stations taking advantage of the change in technology and social trends for mobile over fixed line telephony.

Reviewing where a business delivers value is an important review process, which identifies what and how customers value what your business delivers. By looking at primary activities, those which customers and channel partners directly experience, compared to those which support the business, the secondary, infrastructure elements the opportunity to identify where value is added and where it is not can be identified and assessed. This is not only about focusing on absolute value, is it worth having resources here, or is there another way of doing it, for example insurance used to be provided by salesmen who would visit each home, today it is all done online (as is nearly all music, and many other non-involved and low-value purchases.

Does a business need sales people? Does it need to make it itself or can it outsource that operation? Why is it running its own logistics rather than letting an expert deliver that element of its service? To each of these areas in the value chain the leadership team should be looking at why they are investing in undertaking that activity and not looking at the alterative options in delivering that service and secondly how should that service be delivered.

To give just one simple example of how this model should be used effectively let's think of a brand which designs, makes something and then sells it to retailers. If the leadership assesses that the value is in design, controlling the product and in how the product is being sold to customers, then the question which should be asked is there real value in being a manufacturer. For many premium brands the answer is yes there is, because the manufacturing is an integral part of the value upon which the brand value is developed. But for a growing number of brands, even premium brands from watches to sunglasses the brand name matters, where it is made (and by whom) does not.

When you are undertaking an assessment of the value chain remember that rubbish in will always lead to rubbish out. An assessment needs to be objective and the weakness of letting vested parties undertaking their own assessment will leave the process open to abuse, remember turkey don't vote for Christmas, nor will people in charge of a department provide purely objective assessment of the value they add.

To achieve an honest assessment the leadership team needs to think strategically long-term, discuss their value added processes with key opinion leaders within their market and honestly assess the strengths and weaknesses. The most effective way to reduce them down into three groups of competency

Core Competency 3C model.

When looking at what are the organizations' strengths using the models above should identify to the leadership team the key strengths and weaknesses from an objective macro point of view, the S7 model; from a value added point of view using Porter's value chain using both efficiency and effectiveness measures.

If you look at these objectively they can be summarized into three groups:-

1. **Co-operation**
2. **Customer focused**
3. **Competiveness**

Where does the company internally co-operate successfully, which provides it with a competitive advantage? Where does the company's customer focus give it a competitive advantage and finally where does compete successfully to win business?

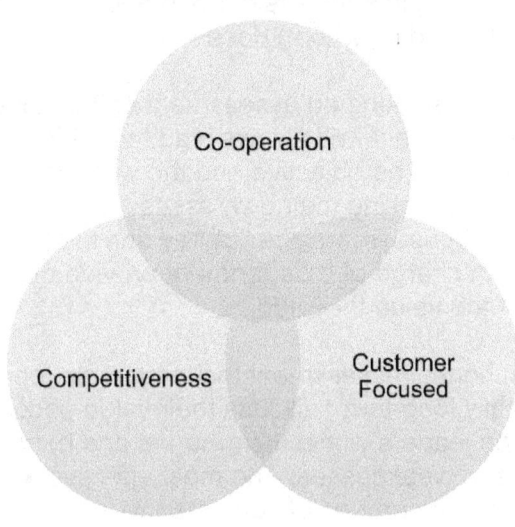

3C model
Richard Gourlay

This summary is a useful way of thinking of a company's core competencies, its strengths and by definition its weaknesses. These are the basis of your internal assessment of your organization.

Chapter 14   SWOT Analysis and TOWS Determination

SWOT Analysis is a well-known and important strategic tool. It provides an understanding of any organizations' internal Strengths and Weaknesses, and for identifying both the Opportunities open to the leadership to take and the Threats they face in taking their business forward. Being well known does not make it less valuable and leadership teams need to recognize the true value of using SWOT analysis effectively.

SWOT so WHAT!

I come across leadership teams who have produced a SWOT and know not what to do with it. They parade the glossed up four box document and read it out, then they stop, and I am left to say "so what, how are you going to use it?" That's the primary problem with strategic planning, people like doing pieces and then stopping. Therefore having crunched the data and produced the information they stop and just stare at it, don't know what to do with it and then file it away in a glossy report and get back to the day job of just surviving.

A good SWOT analysis should be used in conjunction with a TOWS analysis to identify how to proceed strategically. It is about the quality of what you put in that determines what you get out. For that to be successful treating the SWOT analysis as an important asset is an essential first element for its success, but only if it is used effectively to make decisions does it provide real value in determining where to take your business?

The SWOT

A SWOT analysis supports the analysis of the leadership team to identify a sustainable position in any market. It is a summary of the internal business as stakeholders and its external market opportunity as they see it. What makes SWOT particularly powerful is that, with a little thought, it can help the leadership team uncover opportunities that they are well placed to exploit. Furthermore, it enables the leadership team to understand the weaknesses of their business, and develop risk management strategies to manage and eliminate threats that would otherwise damage the business.

The most important element of the SWOT analysis is that by looking at the organization and its competitors using the SWOT framework, the leadership team and stakeholders can formulate a strategy that distinguishes the business from competitors, by playing to its strengths and opportunities so that the business can compete successfully in your market.

Created by Albert Humphrey in the 1960s, this 50-year model combines both an internal assessment of perceived strengths and weaknesses (note the word perceived). This internal analysis offers great insights into the organization; the most effective insights are when the team analyzing the SWOT is a diverse cross section of the company, able to see the whole picture. You are looking for key elements in a SWOT, not an exhaustive list; five good elements are far better than 20 random thoughts. The typical questions to ask in analysing any organization include:-

SWOT Assessment

Strengths
6. What advantages does your organization have within its market?
7. What do you do better than anyone else?
8. What unique or lowest-cost resources can you draw upon that others can't?
9. What do people in your market see as your strengths?
10. What factors mean that you "get the sale"?
11. What is your organization's unique selling proposition (USP), why do people buy from you not someone else?

Notes: Consider your strengths from both an internal perspective, and from the point of view of your customers and people in your market, channel partners, agents and other stakeholders. One useful idea I use with leadership teams is to look at their business in relation to their competitors. How does your business successfully differentiate itself within its market, is a useful tool to identify key strengths.

Weaknesses
- What do you not do well in your team's eyes as a business?
- What could you improve in your customer's views?
- What areas of business do you avoid?
- What do customers in your market see as weaknesses?
- What factors lose you sales?

Notes: Look at weaknesses from an internal and external basis: do other people seem to perceive weaknesses that you don't see? How are your competitors doing any better than you? An honest approach is important for leaders to understand, no business can be good at everything, so produce a concise list of your key weaknesses.

Opportunities
f) What good opportunities from your PESTLE analysis have you identified?
g) What interesting trends are you aware of within your market; see 5 Forces analysis for information?
h) Where is the growth coming from for your customers?
i) What second bounce opportunities are emerging (for example if a new technology has recently been launched, what are the options for new support services to go with it?)
j) What are the diversification options open to you within your markets?

Notes: Opportunities are about the leadership looking at the external market, hence leaders should be looking at their PESTLE analysis as the primary tool for opportunity research. Another area to look at is what customers are looking for to expand or develop the market within which you operate.

Threats
- What external obstacles does you organization face?
- What are your competitors doing, from 5 Forces analysis?
- What changes in regulatory framework could impact upon your business?
- Is changing technology making a step change in the market a threat?
- What new entrants are likely to appear and what market position or customer will they take?

Notes: When looking at opportunities and threats the leadership's PESTLE and 5 Forces analysis provides insight into threats. External threats (avoid the global calamity they need to be realistic and tangible), provides insights for leadership teams as to threats which they can and should plan for.

SWOT template

Strengths	Weaknesses
1.	1.
2.	2.
3.	3.
Opportunities	Threats
1.	1.
2.	2.
3.	3.

A SWOT analysis is a simple but powerful framework for the leadership to analyze its organization's strengths and weaknesses, and the opportunities and threats that it faces. It helps the leadership to focus on its strengths, overcome weaknesses, minimize threats and take the greatest possible advantage of opportunities available to you.

SWOT can also be used to assess competitors and produce a comparative analysis or competing brands.

TOWS

The TOWS analysis can be used instead of SWOT, but actually works as the follow-on from the SWOT. Turning a SWOT into a TOWS analysis turns the information the leadership team has generated into an integrated strategic map of options for the leadership team, how you will win within your market.

A TOWS analysis enables leadership teams to ask the right questions of where the business will operate and which strategies the leadership will pursue.

TOWS answers the following questions:

1. Make the most of your strengths?
2. Circumvent your weaknesses?
3. Capitalize on your opportunities?
4. Manage your threats?

Turning a SWOT (an internal-external analysis) into a TOWS Matrix (the external-internal focused analysis) helps you think about the strategic options that you could pursue.

To do this you match external opportunities and threats with your internal strengths and weaknesses, as illustrated in the matrix below:

TOWS	External Opportunities (O)	External Threats (T)
	1. 2. 3. etc	1. 2. 3. etc
Internal Strengths (S) 1. 2. 3. etc	(SO)Maxi-maxi Strategies play to the organizations key strengths and opportunities	(ST) Maxi-mini Strategies that use strengths to minimize threats
Internal Weaknesses (W) 1. 2. 3. etc	(WO) Mini-maxi Strategies that minimize weaknesses by taking advantage of opportunities.	(WT) Mini-mini Strategies that minimize weaknesses and avoid threats.

TOWS Matrix 1982
H.Weihrich, Ph.D.

For the TOWS analysis to be successful the leadership team needs to look at multiple strategies across the TOWS four options to create good strategic plan:

The use of TOWS enables leadership teams to identify strategic alternatives that address the following additional questions:
- Strengths and Opportunities (SO) – How can you use your strengths to take advantage of the opportunities?
- Strengths and Threats (ST) – How can you take advantage of your strengths to avoid real and potential threats?
- Weaknesses and Opportunities (WO) – How can you use your opportunities to overcome the weaknesses you are experiencing?
- Weaknesses and Threats (WT) – How can you minimize your weaknesses and avoid threats?

The high growth analysis quadrant area SO (maxi-maxi strategies) is always the most appealing. High growth strategies are appealing to stakeholders, often the big hitters or described as game changers, but they need to be supported across the whole spectrum of strategic choices within WO and ST quadrants to convert and minimize the organization from weaknesses and threats. The WT quadrant (weaknesses and threats) is concerned with purely defensive strategies. These are needed to protect the organization from loss, but they will not create success.

Once the TOWS analysis has been completed the leadership team has its strategic map of alternatives, they need to be reviewed to see which strategic options achieve your growth requirements and that best achieve the mission and vision of your organization. Balancing growth across all four quadrants is usually seen as the most responsible and effective strategic decision for the leadership to make.
The TOWS analysis provides simple clarity with a robust methodology behind it which enables leadership teams to analyse the whole strategic playing field to take advantage of the opportunities open to the organization to grow and develop, while simultaneously minimizing the impact of weaknesses and protect

yourself against threats.

These strategies then provide the basis for your business growth.

Chapter 15   Strategic Selection

Selecting business strategy is not a case for leaders doing what they've always done, and just doing it better or harder. It is the case of looking at where the leadership team wants to compete within the market they have chosen. By working out your strategic options by analyzing the external market driver factors and the internal market characteristics coupled with your competitive capabilities, a leadership team can understand the options as to where the leadership wants to compete, and how.

In every market every player has a market position within it. No matter how fleeting every brand has a position compared to another. While these are always changing as companies find, define and continually redefine their competitive edge and meet customers' needs better than the next company. Every market also has its own unique level of competiveness, which can be seasonal, or cyclical, which drives it forward, making the market a sustainable definable one.   The degree of competitiveness between the players within any market, its structure is therefore a reflection of the competitiveness within it. So how companies compete make and define any market. Change in the competitive nature between players within a market changes the market structure and dynamics ot markets.

The leadership of any company has to define how does it gain competitive advantage over other players within a market. Every company looks at competing with players who are direct competitors within their market. Typically competing is about targeting specific customers who a company is trying to win over a small group of competitors who compete with them, where brands provide similar products. Tactical competition, fighting category by category against a competitor may produce marginal success, and a sales manager's role is about identifying where to win with target customers, but no matter how talented the sales unit is it will not drive success unless there is a defined strategy, which the whole company is following.

The only three big picture strategic positions that any company can occupy which Michael Porter identified as his generic competitive business strategies.

1. **Cost leadership.**
2. **Product or Service differentiation.**
3. **Focused segmentation.**

Porter's Generic Strategies: Creating and Sustaining Superior Performance (1985)

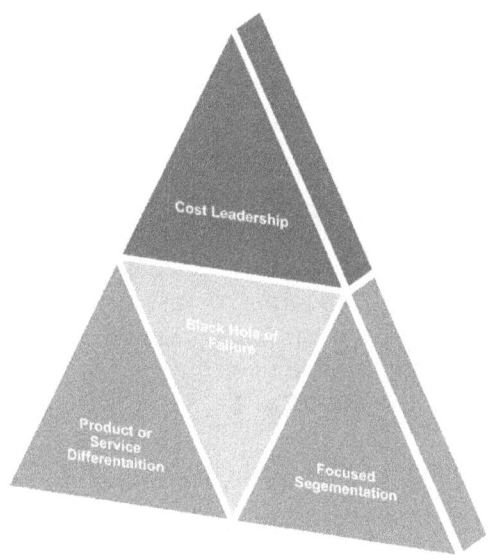

These generic strategies represented the only three ways in which any organization can compete within its market, either on price (lowest cost), on perceived value (differentiation), or by focusing on a very specific customer audience (focused segmentation).

These are the ONLY three strategic options open to the leadership to take with their business. The principle behind these strategic positions is that by focusing the entire business thinking towards one of the three strategic options; Cost leadership, the minimizing of cost to compete within a market; Differentiation, creating uniquely desirable products and services which make the brand distinctly identifiable within its market and Focused Segmentation, by offering a specialized service in a niche market, pure specialization within a market.

Porter's generic strategies are ways of gaining competitive business advantage within any market.

What makes any business competitive within its market is how well it orientates its resources towards a defined position within its market.

Strategic Positions

1. Cost leadership strategy

Cost leadership is about minimizing the cost to the organization of delivering products and services. The Cost Leadership strategy involves being the leader in terms of cost in your industry or market. Being the lowest cost player requires the leadership to focus on removing all possible costs throughout the business to provide the competitive advantage.

1. Cost leadership is not about being cheap, this strategy it is about either:-

   1. Increasing profits by reducing costs, while charging industry-average prices, through aggressive and continual cost reduction.
   2. Increasing market share through charging lower prices, while still making a market acceptable profit on each sale because you've reduced costs.

Unless the leadership can remove costs below everyone else and transfer that into a discernable saving, it cannot use cost leadership as a strategic advantage. The difficulty in cost leadership is in how that conflicts with the value the brand has or offers customers. Removing value changes the strategic position of the brand in everything it does, from how it operates, what it delivers and who it operates with and will always cause problems of retention of key customers.

For cost leadership strategy to succeed it is not just about removing the high cost areas but continually and revolutionary reviewing and reducing all costs to become and retain that low cost strategy being viable.

Capital, logistics, design, manufacturing, support, sales and marketing can all be changed, but the greatest risk in pursuing a cost leadership strategy is that these sources of cost reduction are not unique to you and can quickly be copied. The leadership moving its sourcing to one low cost outsource country, can not only be copied but can be trumped by a competitor finding a lower cost souring country, and therefore this (like every other strategy) requires the leadership to adopt the philosophy of continuous improvement to sustain its advantage.

It is not just new start-ups that can be low cost business models, although it is easier from a blank piece of paper. By using channels like the Internet and outsourced production supported by fulfillment houses, established businesses can follow this strategy through re-invention of existing models

2. Differentiation Strategy

Differentiation is defined as making your products or services different from and more attractive than those of your competitors. In many markets, similar brands compete on a differentiation model. This identification handle enables industrics to be clearly identified as a sector or industry.

Differentiation as a strategy works through familiarity to target audiences, meaning that similar products can compete within defined parameters, white goods for example are generically all the same (not just white) in look. They will all fit into the same kitchen spaces, but each brand has its own identity from which it differentiates itself from others. From fast food outlets to supermarkets, from heavy engineering companies to emergency agencies all identify themselves as part of an industry, a simple clear familiarity handle which can be easily recognized.

The strategy of differentiation is most effective in mature markets where there are established players in a defined market. It requires the leadership to invest in marketing and internal communications to succeed by protecting the defined differentiation position within its market.

Differentiation is therefore a safe model to operate within to gain industry recognition, but it requires brands to differentiate in areas of specialization. For example there are few 3-wheel cars, because the perception of 4 wheels is the industry perception of a car, supported by legislation and convention, yet within the industry the players fight tooth and nail over technology and branding within those parameters.

For a differentiation strategy to succeed, the leadership team must agree that it can and will compete successfully using defined differentiation within its market. It can only do that if it invests in high-quality products and services supported by good research and development, supported by good marketing and sales to drive the differentiation in and across markets.

The second risk for the leadership in pursuing a strategic differentiated strategy is that unless organization stay agile in developing new products and services competitors can outcompete them using focused differentiation strategies within market segments. How and what differentiates one brand from another is a complex mixture which begins with the defined strategy for the business.

Most businesses work within this generic strategy area; they play within the same field but differentiate themselves through their marketing.

3. Focus Segmentation / Niche

By focusing on one particular area of a market the leadership of a company can concentrate and take ownership of that on particular niche market. Becoming a pure specialist within a defined field a company can carve out a definable and defendable position which is clearly outside the way other players who provide that solution operate.

To succeed through focused segmentation a company has to gain specialist expertise within that market that focuses its expertise to solve a particular problem for a specific target audience. In doing so that expertise provides the company with a defensive focused position within the market. Typically in mature high value markets where serving customers command premiums, but requires specific added value, such as luxury goods, are markets where a focused segmentation strategy works particular well. Specific high value demands upon brands operating in markets, for example where relationships and outstanding service are central to the customers' expectations, focused brands build a deep and unique understanding of customer needs and build high value brand loyalty amongst their customers. This makes their particular market segment less attractive to competitors and they are impossible for lower cost operators to enter, making them sustainable as markets mature.

I believe there are four main drivers enabling focused niche strategy to succeed:-

1. Demand for relentless improvement in innovation in product and service by customers.
2. Long-term strategic insight (PESTLE) as to the sustainability of entering a focused market.
3. A passion for innovation and efficiency, which drives people to drive their organization to innovate and improve all aspects of their business
4. Co-operation in driving an industry forward, from staff to customers, channel partners to other stakeholders to succeed exist within that strategic arena.

Without these four drivers focused segmentation is not a successful strategy to adopt.

As markets mature fewer and fewer players, who control and rationalize any market, dominate them. This long-term structural changes to any market swallow up players without a clearly defined strategy. So what makes any strategy and particularly a focused strategy sustainable in the long-term is its ability to sustain.

AT Kearney identify 9 niche sustainable areas and identified successful niche strategies, each are most effective at particular phases of industry consolidation and all built upon the four principles of niche above.

Firstly the Regional niche player, identified as having a solid understanding of customers in a clearly defined regional market.

The second is a focused Target group; which targets certain specific customer segments and deliver extensive personalized services, such as luxury goods, from Rolls Royce to bespoke holidays.

The third is the Product focus; Companies that excel at providing a specific product, for examples such as TiVo and Bang and Olufsen are examples of pure technology focus.

The fourth niche is Branding and lifestyle; Luxury labels focus on target audience as niche drivers of demand who value the brand name such as Harley Davison or Porsche.

The fifth is Speed and lightning consolidation; the rate of change allows innovative niche businesses to become established, such as those from technology companies like Apple and high fashion brands.

The sixth strategy niche is innovation; a business that keeps innovating, that invests in revolution within its market, as I like to call it, can retain a position as a niche player if it can continually re-invent itself. Companies like Google make more money from innovation than from their core tool, Apple imitators like XIOMI are also highly innovative and companies in the technology field often retain their innovation niche through acquisition.

The seventh niche strategy is Cooperation; By forming strategic alliances small companies can compete against large-scale leaders. Farmers' Co-operative, such as Agribbean Agribusiness enables the Caribbean islands to compete in supplying bananas globally.

The eighth niche strategy Market is strategic splitting. Where there are structural supply chain weaknesses in the value chain, such as shipping to small island communities in coastal Scotland a specialist supplier such as Hebrides Haulage can successfully compete.

The last niche strategy is Counter-niche; Companies exploit the weaknesses or strengths of the sector leaders, for example guerrilla brands aimed at youth markets, from clothing to game brands focus on not being mainstream appealing to those who want to stand-out and being different.

The Black Hole of Strategy

It is the leadership team who must decide where it wants to strategically operate. In my model above there is a fourth area, the middle diamond, the black hole of failure.

The black hole of failure is a market position where no brand wants to be yet all are drawn, by the lack of clear strategic direction.

What draws brands towards the black hole of failure is simply the lack of either commitment to one of the three defined generic strategic areas to operate within, or the poor execution of operating within one of the three strategic areas. Being pulled to the middle is what every brand experiences because the leadership lets it happen (or drives it there). Every director wants to grow and that means trying to appeal to everyone it can within its market.

The black hole of failure is where brands lose their identity as they try to be everything to everyone and end being nothing to anyone.

Growth itself pulls brands to look at expansion options. New leadership or powerful external forces, including shareholders or competitor activity, can drive a business to move from being a defined brand within a market to becoming a meaningless name within a market.

Rover cars for example had been a state owned UK industry, which was privatized, but with Government influence. The demands for it to remain as a major large-scale manufacturer (100,000 cars per year player), by Government was part of the condition which the Phoenix partnership agreed to, (unlike the other contenders who planned to make it a focused brand) required them to play on a global market place with a full range offering.

Trying to do everything, have a full suite of models, stretched the company and pulled it away from its defendable differentiated position to the black hole of failure, trying to be everything to everyone. They are not an isolated example.

The Black hole of Failure

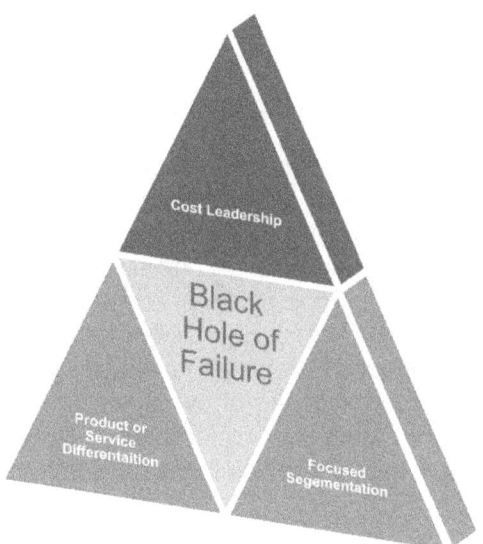

The strategic result of these 'pull forces' is that leadership teams are forced to move from successful areas for their company, into less successful areas and try to become everything to everyone, and that's where they fail. No brand can be everything to everyone, yet leaders want to grow and look to appeal to wider and wider audiences, resulting in weakening their position and ultimately sacrificing their success on the alter of growth. Being pulled to the middle, is effectively strategic failure, no brand can stretch beyond its elastic limit of its brand equity and once its has overstretched itself there is no going back.

Trying to be everything to everyone is caused by leaders not wanting to loose sales and trying to find access to easy growth by selling out their brand for quick (short-term) growth. But once a brand has lost its market position, because someone else will have taken it, it is difficult, if not impossible to regain it. Brands who fall into the black hole always see their market position lost and then their margins are eaten away as they stretch outside their market without the resources to do so which then results in the brand often failing.

Brands being pulled away form a their defined strategic area often see innovation being lost, then they stop competing at the top end of their market, losing their historic premium reducing their average price and ultimately leading to the brand losing its status and becoming an industry label as its brand equity (value) is diminished.

Defining your strategy is the first step in strategic success for any organization.

The sensible way to extend a brand into another market is either to completely reposition it due to long-term strategic needs or to develop a sister brand which specializes within one of the other strategic positions which the leadership wishes to enter. Look at Lexus, Toyota's upmarket brand of car, it is a complete new model aimed at operating in a different market, or BMW's Mini brand, which delivers a premium small car without damaging the BMW brand expectation.

This type of thinking about strategy, the generic approach is vital in setting up a new business, but can be a little too simplistic for leadership teams in established business if it does not define a brand or strategy clearly enough.

To develop your strategic position follow these 3 logical steps:

Step 1 Compare your position to each Strategic Position

For each generic strategy, the leadership team should carry out a S.W.O.T. analysis of your strengths and weaknesses, and the opportunities and threats you would face, if you adopted that strategy.

This should provide the leadership team with a clear strategic fit that the organization is likely or unlikely to be able to make a success within each generic strategy.

Step 2: Analyse the internal forces

By using the 5 Forces Analysis understand the nature of the industry you are in. This will provide a clear picture of your internal market, which will provide an internal view of the markets dynamics and structure.

Step 3: Compare and Contrast

Compare the SWOT Analyses of the viable strategic options with the results of your Five Forces analysis. For each strategic option, ask yourself how you could use that strategy to deal with the 5 forces:

1. Reduce or manage supplier power.
2. Reduce or manage buyer/customer power.
3. Come out on top of the competitive rivalry.
4. Reduce or eliminate the threat of substitution.
5. Reduce or eliminate the threat of new entry.

The most effective generic strategy is one that provides the strongest set of options in dealing with the 5 Forces which internally drive your market.

Bowman's Strategic Clock

To define corporate strategy in a clearer way than Porter's generic 3 strategies, and derivations of it, Bowman and Faulkner developed Bowman's Strategy Clock. This model of corporate strategy extends Porter's three strategic positions to eight, and explains the cost and perceived value combinations which many leadership teams use, as well as identifying the likelihood of success for each strategy.

Bowman's strategic clock defines eight different strategies that are identified by varying levels of price and value as drivers of strategic differentiation.

Bowman's Strategic Clock

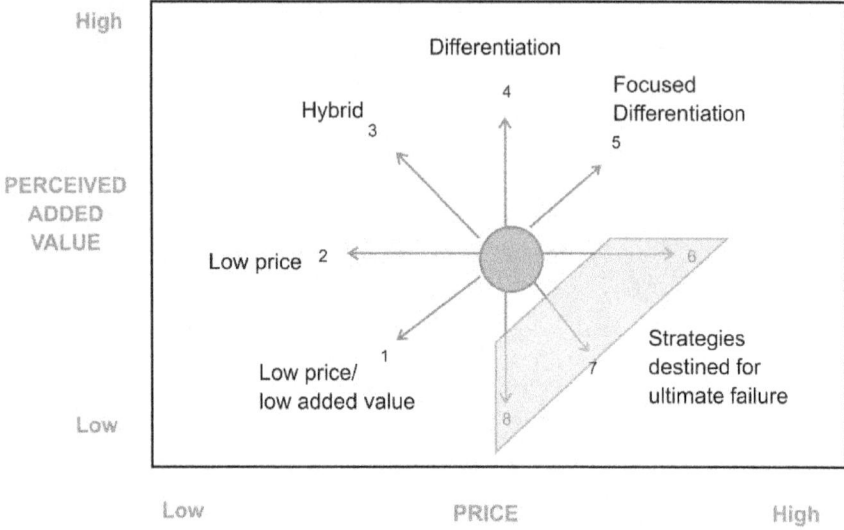

Cliff Bowman and
David Faulkner 1997.

Bowman's clock model shows the impact of price and value as the key drivers of differentiation within any market.

Position 1: Low Price/Low Value

The "bargain basement" a once unpopular area to compete within, is now seen as a lucrative area for many brands, aiming at lower economic target audiences and is also a useful online model. From German food retailers to DIY retailers and value retailers (Poundland and 99p stores), these non-differentiated brand companies utilize logistical efficiency and narrow range of generic product to take the low-price/ low-cost strategic position.

Own brand labels, and white labeled goods protect margin, low cost sites and stack them high sell it cheap appeals to cost conscious customers.

Position 2: Low Price

The second position is where the leadership decides to compete as a low cost leader. These companies drive prices down to bare minimums, and they balance very low margins with very high volume. Typically they are large volume sales companies or strong strategic reasons for their position, by sustaining this approach they become a powerful force in their market.

Walmart is a key example of a low price competitor that persuades suppliers to enter the low price arena with the promise of extremely high volumes. Brands in this clock position often use loss leaders to generate sales and have recognized branded product sprinkled amongst value for money and own brand budget products.

Position 3: Hybrid Position (moderate price/moderate differentiation)

The hybrid market position is where companies offer products at a low cost through price incentivized selling, while offering products with a higher perceived value than those of other low cost competitors. This position requires volume, which is driven through brand reputation of offering fair prices for reasonable goods. The quality and value is good and the consumer is assured of reasonable prices. This combination builds customer loyalty; this is where mainstream retailers across most retail sectors operate, working in the mass market driving growth through price through focused customer loyalty schemes.

Position 4: Differentiation

Pure differentiation is achieved through differentiate offer their customers through high perceived-value. This is achieved by either using increasing price to support higher margins, or they keep their prices low and seek greater market share. Differentiation is about the use of the brand identity as the strategy as it allows a company to become synonymous with quality as well as a price point. Iconic brands like Airstream and Amazon are great examples of differentiated brands.

Position 5: Focused Differentiation

Focused differentiation, is where the leadership team determines to focus the brand at target audiences who will buy in this brand based on perceived value alone. The product or service does not necessarily have to have any more real value, but the perception of value is enough to charge very large premiums. By focusing on key attributes such as brand heritage, distribution, or promotion a business can focus its strategy to those who will pay for the premium of that brand.

Ideal target markets for focused differentiation products and services are the luxury goods sectors in virtually every market.

Luxury goods are often multiple times more in price than non-luxury models and play on their heritage, their pedigree or their promotion focused towards a defined regional or global target audience.

Position 6: Increased Price/Standard Product

A temporary strategy, which companies can adopt, is to increase price. This non-sustainable strategy can be a result of competitor failure or as a result of sudden market condition changes, which allow a company to increase price without any other changes. These opportunistic companies look to respond to scarcity or turbulent market conditions to increase margins.

While this strategy is appealing, and sometimes it can be continued for a period of time, it is an unsustainable position for any company to adopt. Many brands try this model when they can, scarcity is the prime driver, like a taxi late at night, but it is ultimately not sustainable.

Position 7: High Price/Low Value

The ability to charge a high price for a low value, an oxymoron in any open market does exist where monopoly industries exit.

Monopoly pricing is only an option where the company has exclusivity of supply, or distribution. In open market economies monopolies do not last very long, except in state provided services, where single entities, monopolies, are protected to provide a single service. Due to globalization these are becoming fewer as barriers, costs and market conditions change.

Position 8: Low Value/Standard Price

The race to the bottom market position is one where only price lets a product sell. While every company has products to get rid of, it is unsustainable to have a fire sale every day. The old quote, if you are not adding value get out has never been truer of this market position.

If you are not adding value get out!

The closing down sale may generate sales but it is never going to build a business!

Summary

Selecting your strategic position for a new company or in developing a future position for your company is an essential element for success. Of all the positions which Bowman's strategic clock provides, the final three positions on Bowman's clock are the non-viable competitive strategies in truly competitive marketplaces.

If ever price is greater than perceived value the leadership team has to recognize they are in an unsustainable position. There will always be competitors offering better quality products at lower prices so leaderships have to ensure that value and price are aligned correctly.

Bowman's Strategic Clock focuses on the relationship between price and value.

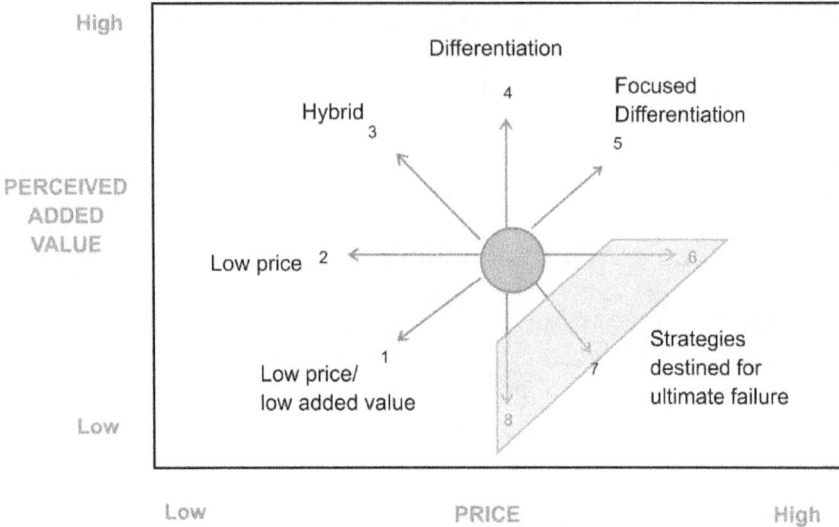

The best way to utilize it to determine your optimum strategic position beyond the generic model is to think through the following questions, starting from the centre point of the Clock, work outwards using the questions below:-.

Leadership questions to determine brand perceived value:
1. How much does your product or service offering enable you to charge a premium price within the market? (High, move up: low move down)
2. How well defined is your target market? (High move up and right: if low move up and left)
3. How well is the target market's value stream aligned with the brand offering? (High move upwards and right: if low move up and left)
4. Is the brand differentiation clear and defendable? (If high move up and right: if low then move up and left)
5. Does the brand have multiple points of differentiation to sustain competitive advantage in the market? (High, move up: low move down)

Leadership questions to determine brand price:

1. How much control do you have over costs to sustain a good margin? (High, move right, if not move left).

2. Can costs be actively managed to gain advantage? (High, move left, if not move right)
3. Can you balance low price against the perception of low value? (High, move right: if not move left)
4. Are cost advantages limited to one or a few small market segments? (High, move left down, if not move right up)
5. Are target segments capable of sustaining the business model? (High, move right, if not move left)

This model provides a more defined strategic model than the over simplistic Porter 3 position. For any business deciding where to play, its generic strategy is based upon your core competency model of what it does well as a business. If the generic strategy and core competencies conflict, then by definition your chances of success will be limited. By aligning your generic strategy with your core competencies, the resources you have available to you, the environment in which you operate and any market expectations you have already established then leadership teams can identify their optimum strategic business within their market.

This is an effective way of looking at how to establish and sustain a competitive position in any market driven economy. By applying these two sets of questions leadership teams can define which of the eight basic strategic positions best fits with their competency and opportunity. For an established business leadership teams can analyze and evaluate their current strategy and determine if adjustments might improve your overall competitive position.

Chapter 16   Strategic Models

Strategy is no substitute for vision for a leader, but vision without a strategy to deliver it is just a dream. While strategy enables leaders to see how to proceed, it does not give them the end purpose; it may explain what is changing in the sector, but a strategy needs to have a purpose to make it live. Without a vision, a leader's future aspiration for their organization, there is no purpose to where they are going. With no vision an organization has no forward view of the world within which it operates.

Developing your strategy is therefore an essential requirement for successfully defining your vision. This tangible link between vision and strategy is one of the missing links, which leaders often fail to make. It is relatively easy to come up with a vision if you step back from being inside your business for long enough, but is the vision…

Worth pursuing?
Realistic?
Deliverable?
Workable?
Sellable to your stakeholders?

A vision that answers these questions successfully is one that is built upon solid foundations. To be able to answer those questions with certainty, leaders need to focus on the credibility of the information leaders look to for sources of data. The critical element therefore in building a successful vision, supported by a deliverable strategy, is information. Looking for and finding reliable sources of data is vital. **Definitions of strategic analysis often differ, but the following attributes are commonly associated with it:**

1.   Identification and evaluation of data relevant to strategy formulation.
2.   Definition of the external and internal environment to be analysed.

3. A range of analytical methods that can be employed in the analysis.

It is important to know what information to look for in the first place and how to filter out the noise of erroneous data, uninformed opinion, not to mention complete lack of information on certain markets. Data is vital to answer:

"Without data you're just another person with an opinion."
W. Edwards Deming

The value of good quality data is that it provides reliable information upon which intelligence about future opportunities can be drawn. Strategy is often perceived as a route to take, but actually strategy delivers more to leaders, from a direction and focus through to a plan that can be interrogated and used to gain support from stakeholders. The value of developing your strategy is that it gives leaders....

"an integrated set of choices that uniquely positions the firm in its industry, so as to create sustainable advantage and superior value relative to the competition." Lafley and Martin
The decision-making process, which leaders have to go through, should be designed and focused around delivering the outcome. The objective of defining an organizations unique position (a defendable one) is essential in strategy selection. The set of choices that leaders have to make should be a logical hierarchy of steps and can often be seen as a framework of decisions leaders can use to select the right strategic approach for their organization. They can then make operational choices that support this strategy.

Lafley and Martin's framework to develop a winning strategy looks to answer five questions in descending order:

1. What is our winning aspiration?
2. Where will we play?

3. How will we win?
4. What capabilities must we have in place to win?
5. What management systems are required to support our choices?

Lafley and Martin 5 Step Strategy Model

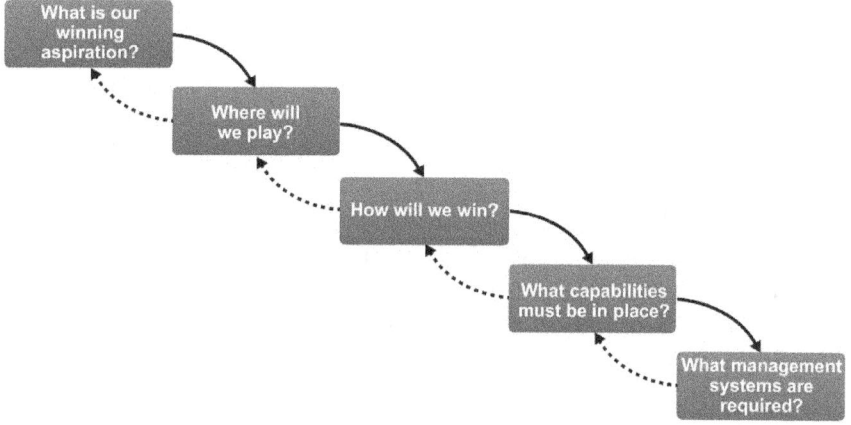

1. What is our winning aspiration?

First step, the winning aspiration is all about the vision you as the leader have about your organization. Defining where you want go is not just about being number 1, it is about where does the leadership team (or leader) see the business within the next 1, 3 or 5 years.

Typically when a new CEO is given the role in a large company they have the honeymoon period of 3 months or 10 days to come up with their vision, their aspiration and the plan to deliver it.

2. Where will we play?

The second element of this framework is where we will play. This challenges the leadership team to work out what and where the opportunities lie. This requires the use of tools and techniques to see how and what changes are likely to occur within your chosen market and how your organization can take advantage of those changes.

3. How will we win?

The third part of the framework is that defining point of any strategy, how will we win. This is the most important question, which any leader must be able to articulate. Why should someone buy from us rather than someone else? It is probably the single most asked question I ask leaders. Not just because it is the most valuable question but it also demonstrates how much investment has been made in working on their business. How will we win, is the point of the strategy, its sharp end and the tangibility which leaders must be able to convey. In every business knowing your competitive advantage and how it is being used to win business is important.

This is the central pillar of the strategy and from it every department and everyone within it needs to be able to understand. This central part of the strategy has to be at the heart of how the strategy will live.   Everything that happens to make the strategy happen, the action plan, has to focus on this key element. All the actions must link back to this key element. For example, if you are providing a product on a short turnaround, from fast food through to shipping, and speed is your key 'win factor' it must be central to the whole ethos of what you are delivering.

This point is central to success because it allows every department and person to become involved with the strategy. Every department must bring the strategy to life by making the appropriate changes to deliver the strategy.

4. What capabilities must we have in place to win?

What does it take to deliver the intended win? What needs to change and when? Who is going to do what differently to produce the results you need to achieve? The answer to this point of creating the implementation plan is to start by looking at what you have already in place, something I call the 3C's (Competencies, Capabilities and Competitiveness) which will have informed your winning aspiration at point 1 in the framework and then look for the gaps. Where do we need new capabilities requires an objective look at the whole picture of what the organization does and what it needs to do to outcompete its competition.

One mistake many leaders make is in assuming that just being better is good enough. The competition benchmarking approach of what number 1 at the subject is 'where we need to be' used to be seen as the easiest way to become better than them. This is an excellent first stage assessment of current expectations, but it assumes everyone will sit still while you develop your strategy. No business lives in a vacuum, and likewise while you are developing your strategy, so is everyone else.

Frank Dick, who from 1979 to 1994 was the British Athletics Federation's Director of Coaching, led the British Athletics team into its "golden era" with Olympic gold medallists such as Daley Thompson, Steve Ovett and Sebastian Coe. He describes the process of capability development in a very simple way. If you are the manager of a football team who is down one nil at half time, how many goals do you need to win in the second half? The obvious answer is two, but the real answer is three, because your competitor is going to expect you to score a goal to get the draw, so they are going out in the second half to get a second goal to secure the win, so if you want to win you will need to score three goals to win.

This understanding of step change is important, just benchmarking, a good first start but only that, lets you see how any business has been successful in getting where they are. But it will not tell you how they will compete tomorrow.

Resourcing capability is an essential component in any strategy. You can't make anything new happen without the resources, from people and processes, through to skills and actions.

5. What management systems are required to support our choices?

To deliver your strategy successfully, it will only happen if every department does its part. Having the right management systems in place is vital for success. It will require changes to be made. For a strategy to succeed it will require new systems to be introduced.

To make a step change happen will always require new management systems. The old adage:

"The definition of insanity: doing the same thing time and time again and expecting a different result."

Even if a division within the organization is fit for purpose to deliver the strategy, pulling the division together and the whole organization forward will always require everyone making change.

Management systems enable step change to happen. New management systems are an integral part of action planning which delivers the implementation of a new strategy.

Chapter 17   The Importance of Goal Setting

One of the first things I do when I sit down with leaders to discuss strategy is always to ask them how will they measure the success of their strategy.

Business owners of every type of business understand the importance of measuring what matters. Everyone measures some areas of their business; turnover is the easiest and most recognizable measurement every business has. Even when I first meet a business owner they will share their turnover (if it is worth measuring), or the growth of it, we are X% up on last year.

Having clear goals are vital if you want to bring a strategy to life. The challenge is that most strategic thinking is about a position in a market, 'to be the premium brand in the market' for example, but leaders struggle to turn aspirational words into numerate goals and objectives. If you challenge them they might have an aspiration of their target market. Leaders only like to numerate their goals once they have achieved them. The irony is that without goals you cannot achieve them. It's not a chicken and egg question it is about being positive, focused and committed to what you are aiming at.

Strategic goals are about numerating what you want to achieve. I often phrase this to leaders by saying you can't be a little bit pregnant, you either are or you aren't committed to it, and that commitment is made up of how you numerate your strategy.

A strategy only works when leaders commit to convert thinking and words into what they are going to accomplish by turning it into targets that people can hit. That brings your plan to life to everyone within your organization.

Business owners should not fear setting goals or objective projections because there is no downside to doing so. Many will tell you they don't want to internally publicize their plan, in case it does not turn out as to how they planned. In many ways it is like trying to be a little bit pregnant, you want the new offspring to just appear out of nowhere. If you won't commit to objectives and goals for your strategy then you will certainly succeed in not achieving your goals.

The best strategies are not about turnover revenues; turnover is an outcome of a strategy it rarely tells you anything useful about launching a new strategy for your business.

For example entering a new market needs objectives built around market entry measurements, who specifically is your target audience and what are your measurable goals that you can measure towards the goal of doing business with them?

That sales pipeline measurement is a vital tool to create reality in succeeding with entering a new market. If you only measured the end sales your strategy would fail before you succeed. Measuring the right stuff is vital for strategies to succeed. Something new always requires bespoke measurements to provide supporting evidence of being on the right track, or if you are not.

Here are my four reasons why you should be setting strategic goals for your organization:

1. Measure Success

Good organizations should always be trying to improve, grow, and become more profitable. Setting strategic goals provides the clearest way to measure the success of the company's new strategies.

When you are looking at your company from a one to five year perspective, you are looking beyond the tactical side of your business (short term success, measured by weekly and monthly sales) and instead taking a much more macro view, which allows you to see the company from a competitive, business vertical or economic perspective. This is where key tools such as balanced scorecard measurements become very important.

2. Creating Strategic Team Cohesion

Setting strategic goals ensures that everyone understands what the real prize is and what they are working towards. When your leadership team clearly understands what you are trying to accomplish with your strategy it provides the rationale for the decisions you might make regarding hiring, firing, promoting restructuring, or any other decisions. This transparency of clear goals and objectives enables people to trust where they are going so it helps support the cohesion of the team because it allows everyone to pull in the same direction. Think about Maslow's hierarchy of needs, people have to trust their work environment to perform well; otherwise they start acting in a protective internalizing way.

If people are off delivering a specific element of the strategy, other people feel comfortable in people undertaking unusual activities as long as those people come back and report against a known target. If people have no target to hit and nothing to report back against, then people do not trust what is going on.

If your whole team, from the leadership colleagues down, can see where you are going then they can understand why you are making those decisions. This eliminates a lot of the uncertainty that goes with not understanding the goals of the company.

3. Knowledge Is Power

When your goals have been defined, you can develop a deeper understanding of the effects of tactical decisions and how they play against the strategic goals. Without clear goals you have no knowledge of if your strategic plan is working. How without clear goals can you measure success of doing something new? Setting clear goals and objectives sets a benchmark, a model of expectation, ultimately giving your knowledge, particularly important when looking at doing something new.

Clear goals enable people to make informative decisions, which are not based and biased, subjective in nature. Leaders moving out of their comfort zone, starting something new, launching a new strategy need to define what good looks like as numbers rather than perceptions. Setting goals is a clear way to convert your knowledge into real power.

4. Goal Assessment

When you set out goals in launching your strategy you can review your strategy throughout the plan, do and review cycle. Being able to respond positively and early with confidence requires having tangible evidence, evidence which can be observed by all and reviewed to make informed decisions by. This allows a quicker and agreed change of course in response to what is happening, because they have a factual base to make decisions from.

For example, if your strategy is to open up 20 new customers from a new service, even if everyone loves the new service but midway through the first quarter you find that your financial projections for this service are not tracking like you had expected. If you have objective measurements throughout the launch of the strategy not related to revenue then you can objectively see where the strategy was not delivering rather than waiting until the year end and to find that this new service has not delivered.

If you hadn't set the goals, this type of information is not as apparent and decisive action is more difficult. It is incredibly important to remember that setting business goals will not ensure success for any organization. However, there's also a lot to be said for not flying by the seat of your pants. Taking the time to look at your organization from a broader perspective will give you greater confidence in what lies ahead and how your organization will be able to optimize it. We can't predict the future, but we can certainly plan for it.

Why Goals Matter in Strategy

Goals not only carry people with you for launching and delivering your strategy, but also enable strategic assessment to be compared. In a fight for scarce resources, being able to measure requires strategy to include setting clear objectives and goals. Setting objectives towards goals, enables a strategy to live, it enables everyone involved to know the steps to success and their role in delivering that success.

Goal outcomes, things we achieve like getting an appointment, matter because they are milestones to demonstrate success.

Without goals and objectives a strategy is unlikely to succeed because there are not measures of success. Whether you hit or miss a target is not as important as having a target. The very fact of having a target creates a far higher chance of hitting that target. I often explain to people who resist goal setting in their strategy that like a golfer you miss every shot you do not take, likewise with strategy if you don't set targets how you do you know if it is working and how well. If you don't know you are being measured how will you know you are doing it right?

Chapter 18   What major problems does your business address for your target audiences?

One of the major challenges that any strategic plan needs to focus on, and any leader working on the plan needs to focus on, is 'it's not just what you do' that your customers buy. Often people focus around the key products or services that companies sell. Actually, why your customers buy from you is vital to understand so that you can understand how you add real value to your customers and why they buy from you and not from somebody else in solving their problems; and that is one of the key things that any strategic plan needs to focus around. One of your key competencies in front of your customers is actually what people do when they buy from you. One of the things I find with clients is how little clients actually know about why their customers buy from them. Often, leaders and Directors of businesses are focused around the key bit they do, in terms of the products or services they are focused on, and they don't look at the whole reason people buy from them.

So what are the underlying reasons why people buy from you? It could be about where you started from as a business, how you deliver the service, what you actually do that makes a bigger value to the customer than just the core product.

I have always found that in terms of what I do, it is the width of my experience and my knowledge and my ability to come up with practical solutions, which makes me, stand out from other people.

What problem are you solving which is often not related to what you do? When I used to work for Berghaus, one of the things which my customers said to me was that they really also valued me for my business advice. You know what is going on and you understand how to engage with customers. That is one of the things that got me in front of people that other people could not get an appointment with.

So when you think around that, developing a successful strategy is not just about playing to your core product or services, but what is the raison d'etre, what's the reasoning behind why people do business with you?

Let me give you a really simple example of this; one of my client bases is accountants and if you ask them what their customers buy from them, one of the reasons accountants give is 'we keep our customers legal'. Well, compliance work to stay legal is the core service that customers pay for but if you sit down with their customers and ask them what they get from their accountants they will give a whole range of things.

When I work with them not understanding their real value to customers is one of their weaknesses in their strategy by not understanding what they could be doing for people. So, for example, not only does an accountant keep you legal by doing compliance work but also accountants understand regulation and how regulations change to do with finance and to do with financial reporting. That type of advice about how to set up, how to run and how to organize becomes really important. If a business has a business idea that involves money, often they come back and talk to their accountant because they trust that accountant and they trust what the accountant is saying. So the accountant as a trusted advisor is one of the reasons why people will invest money in an accountant's services. They are also someone who can help with funding, somebody who understands the process, the routine, and they understand the contacts and the documentation of more than just a business plan.

Those things are part of what makes a financial advisor so important to people as an accountant. They are the person who will probably be working with the Finance Director so they may be involved with helping the Directors with the recruitment of that role. They may also be the person who will help set up the financial system for the business or help with modernization of the system such as new software or IT interfaces with the finance system. So when you now think about what does an accountant actually do for a business you can see it can be so much more than just to keep you legal, it is part of the inner network of advisors who advise the business owners on what they are doing.

So, if a business is going to launch a new strategy, one of the things it would do is bounce the strategy off its accountant to see what their thoughts are.

Accountants by and large look backwards, they look at past performance, but knowing what the company has been good at and how it does it, they will be one of the trusted sources that people focus around in what they are doing. So, one of the things I would suggest any business owner does, and here is a quick suggestion for you, why don't you ask your customers why do they buy from you and not from somebody else? Look beyond the core product or services that they actually buy from you. What else do they get? What do they enjoy about buying from you? Why do you add value that somebody else doesn't?

Peter Drucker who is a fantastic expert in the field of running businesses once said 'what problem are you able to solve rather easily that would be hard for most people to do?' One of the things you could think around that is, actually what do we do for our customers? List out the things that they get but also ask them, particularly the core customers and the ones growing and developing within their markets. What do we give them? What do we provide for them that helps them grow and develop successfully or do more confidently because of their relationship with us? It could be, as for my example with accountants, that they provide that extra backup, that extra advice, that almost non-executive Director role which many businesses have, or that expert in the finance field role they have. Or, it could be in the field that you're in, have a look at what you do beyond your core service. It could be the extra service, it could be the way you deliver it, it could be the innovation that you bring to the market, it could be the trusted relationships your business has. Look for your core competencies with your core customers to understand, actually, what you do for customers in reality. There is a lot more than simply the product or service that they pay upfront for. That will help you understand how you add real value on what you deliver in terms of the value to the customers and to the industry within which you are in. That is an important part of how organizations add value and it is core to understanding if you are going to be competent at things.

What are your core competencies that you can take to market and use to support any strategies that you are developing for your business?

Chapter 19   What Happens Once a Plan is Created?

A key mistake people make here is that people think that the plan being created is the outcome. That is only the start of the process. Action planning is all about turning your plan into outcomes that move people towards the goals. Whether it is making changes internally so that your organization is fit for purpose to achieve your plan or whether it is about undertaking research to identify whether those markets you think are existing are tangible and how best to approach them, action planning is the vital next stage in terms of what you want to do with your plan. Your plan has to have momentum and the planning process and the plan itself is the start of creating that momentum in terms of what you want to achieve. So, creating action plans, working out how to gain buy-in and how to implement your plan is the key outcome once you have actually developed your plan.

How Do I Implement My Business Plan?

Implementing a business plan is firstly a commitment from the leader themselves in believing in the plan. They have to be fully committed and fully believing in the plan they have committed to. That then leads to the stage of starting people to buy in to your plan and actually getting everybody committed to and involved with the plan is important. The first step is always a small step to take and is to get people involved, not just focusing around the eager people, the early adopters, but looking at your majority to see some plan happening, to see some momentum being created. So small steps forward are a vital part of making change happen. So if you want to implement a plan, an action plan that has small steps is a vital part of that. You are looking to get people involved early in making steps that people can see and believe in that actually show progress. Part of that process needs to be involving people, making change and making sure that you are leading people forward and seeing outcomes towards the end goal. Often when you start making change there are very few tangible outcomes that can be seen. So identifying how to create visible outcomes that show capability and competence in what you are doing make a big difference.

Chapter 20   How to make change happen

Leadership's biggest challenge is in implementing strategic change within their organization. Change is the vital element in making things happen, but it is one of the hardest skills and processes to deliver. The problem with change is that it is a simple word to say, but making it happen is probably the hardest activity to achieve in business, or anywhere. Change, the need for change is driven by creating a vision and determining the strategy to achieve it.

When a strategy is being considered, one major consideration I always look at is can this leadership team deliver that strategy. What I am looking at is can they make the required changes within themselves and their organization that will enable them to be fit and able to undertake that strategy.

The answer to the question is always to look at the three 'Cs' how:-

1. **Capable of handling change;** this is the factor to assess of how big a change is needed to be made functionally within the organization. How much effort and leadership resource needs to be invested to achieve the capability to undertake the required change(s). This reflects how much change needs to happen and where, when and how. That requires an assessment of the capability of the organization in undertaking change, which reflects how much and what type of change that organization and people within the organization can successfully handle change. This understanding of capacity to change often reflects the type of organization it is, the nature of the environment and the type and rate of changes it has and is undertaking.

2. **Comfortable with change**; how does the leadership see the required changes to be made, are they comfortable with them themselves. Which is essentially how much do they have to change. Does the leadership team believe in

the change are they comfortable with the changes that need to happen.

I often demonstrate this to people by getting them to think through a change and the benefits it will deliver and ask them to value whether that change is worth the change that they will have to undertake. Then I get them to fold their arms, and then ask them to refold their arms the other/way. Then I ask them how easy was it to make that change, after the fun of trying to change the way they have folded their arms for X number of years, I then ask them to rethink how comfortable they and their organization is with making the proposed changes that they will need to implement.

3. **Competitive with change**; does the leadership value the need for change more than the desire (intransigence / insipidity / resistance) to not change. Everyone says change is easy, until you look at why change is resisted. Change only happens when the need for change powers the competitive requirement within the leadership and is greater than the visible and invisible forces that resist change. Change only happens when the competitive environment within the organization is greater than the forces of resistance to change. This final C combines the power of the vision with the need to make changes within organization's environment.

These three factors will determine the chances of success of making change. This change model has been codified into a simple formula, which shows these factors and the power relationships between them.

The Change Formula

$$\text{Change} = D \times V \times F > R$$

Change equals **Dissatisfaction** X **Vision** X **First Steps** that is greater than the **Resistance.** This model, first attributed to David Gleicher, is that if you are seeking some significant, system-wide change there are core elements that the leadership needs pay particular attention to.

The leadership has to identify and drive beyond the tipping point to create a critical mass within the organization to:

Be **dissatisfied (D)** with the way things are (in direct relationship to the proposed change) is the first stage in change happening. Without dissatisfaction change will never happen. For change to occur either there has to be a direct failure which creates a crisis for the organization, or the leadership has to create a crisis of capability so change can occur. The market changes, new competitor entry or the inability to do something that is now required, regulation changes, customer expectation etc.

To have a **vision (V)**, a clear idea of what a better future or improvement would look like, built and owned by the leadership team, which is communicated by them to the employees and stakeholders. An old saying among leaders is **"Being right is only one-quarter of the battle."** It's not uncommon for leaders to have a vision of what changes are required. The challenge for many leaders is that just communicating the vision alone will not bring change. Any successful vision must be communicated if it is ever to succeed. What makes a best-selling author is not the quality of the writing but the ability of the author to sell it to others.

The **first steps (F)** is a key success factor in making change happen. Creating momentum, even if it is the smallest step (and often the smallest step that everyone takes together within the team). Taking everyone towards that vision requires four major factors for leaders to assess:

1). What competencies need to be developed (or strengthened) for people to be able to function in the changed situation?

2). People are often hesitant to accept and implement the change because they fear the impact of those changes.

3). Having the resources to make the change.

4). Creating the alignment of the structure, process and practices so that they work together.

Managing **Resistance (R)** can only be overcome by the combined weight of the dissatisfaction, vision and first steps overpowering that resistance. That means if any of those elements (D, V, F) is "0", the change will not be possible.

This is where one key additional factor the drive and passion of the leadership to drive through change is about the three 'Cs' I mentioned earlier. One key model in minimising resistance is to adopt the intervention theory by Chris Argyris. This theory promotes the moving of the tipping point of involvement, from a small project team to include more people in the problem throughout the diagnosis and solution development process which reduces resistance and develops enhanced commitment throughout the team.

Leaderships Continual Role to Drive Through Change

The Change Process

There are many different ways to make change happen. In my experience no-one has refined it as well as John Kotter. A professor at Harvard Business School and world-renowned change expert, Kotter introduced his eight-step change process in his 1995 book, "Leading Change."

Step 1: Create Urgency
For change to happen successfully, it needs the whole company to buy-in to it. By developing a sense of urgency around the need

for change coupled with spark the initial motivation to get things moving.

This requires an open, an honest and convincing dialogue about what's happening in the marketplace, the causes and consequences of those changes. If many people start talking about the change you propose, the urgency can build and feed on itself.

First stages to Create Urgency:
- Identify changes in the market (potential threats), and develop scenarios showing the future impact of these changes.
- Examine opportunities that should be, or could be, exploited.
- Start honest discussions, and give dynamic and convincing reasons to get people talking and thinking.
- Request support from customers, outside stakeholders and industry people to strengthen your argument.

Tip:
Kotter defines for change to be successful, **75%** of a company's management needs to "**buy into**" the change. Leadership has to work really hard on Step 1, and spend significant time and energy building an argument for urgency, before moving onto the next steps. Don't move too fast, get buy-in right but don't let it become change stagnated.

Step 2: Form a Powerful Coalition
The leadership must communicate the need to people that change is necessary. This requires strong leadership whose passion and vision drive all the key people within your organization. Managing change isn't what leadership is about; leadership is about leading it. To lead change, create a coalition of influential people whose power comes from a variety of sources, from status, expertise, and political importance.
Once formed, your "change coalition" needs to work as a team, continuing to build urgency and momentum around the need for

change.

Creating a Coalition
- Create a powerful communication narrative to buy people in.
- Identify the true leaders and influencers in your organization, as well as your key stakeholders.
- Ask for an emotional commitment from these key people.
- Lead your team building within your change coalition.
- Check your team and buy-in for weak areas, and ensure that you have a good mix of people from different departments and different levels within your company.

Step 3: Create a Vision for Change
The challenge for leaders in creating your vision for change is that there are many great ideas and solutions floating around. Defining these concepts into an overall vision that people can grasp easily and remember. KISS is an important chestnut (Keep It Simple Stupid) to make a clear vision that everyone can simply understand why you're asking them to do something different.

When people see for themselves what you're trying to achieve, then the directives they're given tend to make more sense.

Steps in Creating a Vision

1. Define the values that are central to the change required.
2. Create a short summary, an elevator pitch (one or two sentences) that captures what you "see" as the future of your organization.
3. Create a strategy to execute that vision.
4. Ensure that your change coalition can describe the vision in five minutes or less.
5. Practice your "vision speech" often.

Step 4: Communicate Your Vision
Using your vision correctly, how you launch it has a disproportionate impact in determining the success of the change

you are going to make. Your vision statement will probably have strong competition from the many other day-to-day communications within the company, so you need to communicate it frequently and powerfully, and embed it within everything that you do.

Present your vision every chance you can. Use the vision to make decisions and be the basis of solving problems. By keeping it fresh on everyone's minds, the team will remember it and respond to it in the way you wish them to.
The leaders must also "walk the talk." What you do is far more important and believable than what you say. Demonstrate the kind of behavior that you want from others and make sure it is seen.

How to Communicate your Vision:
• Talk and visualize your change vision.
• Address peoples' concerns and anxieties, openly and honestly.
• Develop your vision to how it will impact all aspects of the organizations performance; create the change you want to see.
• Tie everything about the future back to the vision you have created.
• Lead by example in making progress to start and be maintained.

Step 5: Remove the Obstacles
Creating momentum for creating and sustaining change is vital for change to happen. The leadership role in removing obstacles is firstly to plan out where obstacles might occur, and what those obstacles will look like. With that knowledge don't get carried away with the emotion of change, working on your business is being able to stay detached enough to see what is going on. Seeing where and what resistance looks like is an essential ingredient, assessing the validity of the resistance and responding with viable answers.

Put in place the structure for change, and continually check for barriers to it. Removing obstacles can empower the people you need to execute your vision, and it can help the change move forward.

How to Remove Obstacles
- Identify, create or recruit change champions whose main roles are to deliver the change.
- Review and refine the organizational structure, job descriptions, and performance and compensation systems to ensure they're inline with your vision.
- Recognize and reward people for making change happen.
- Identify, validate and review resistance and the people who are resisting the change, and help them see what's needed.
- Take action quickly to remove barriers (human or otherwise).

Step 6: Create Short-Term Wins
Nothing succeeds or motivates more than success. Give your company a taste of victory early in the change process; use a quick win to drive success forward that your people can see. Without quick tangible wins, critics and negative thinkers might hurt your progress. Quick wins also enable the silent majority, those people who stay silent, or do not actively engage with change (because it does not impact on them at the initial stages)

Create short-term targets; a good project manager creates and drives people towards clear milestones. Do not rely upon the final state as success, one long-term goal. Successful leadership is about carrying people to each smaller target to be achieved.

How to Create Short-term Wins

1. Look for sure-fire quick wins and clear milestones towards or as part of your vision that you can implement.
2. Choose targets that are low cost, low involvement quick wins. You want to be able to justify the investment in change.
3. Understand the risk profile (cost credibility compared to benefits) of the potential pros and cons of your quick win goals. Pick an early goal, which does not hurt your entire change initiative.

4. Reward through recognition, the people who help you meet those quick wins.

Step 7: Build on the Change

As change starts, many leaders see the process of change beginning to happen as success of their vision and the end of their role in leading change. This is the critical point of failure for making change. Real change is not a movement towards, or away, but the sustainability of the new embedded within the organization. For the leadership to ensure success, continually driving their vision forward is about moving everyone to reach the state where the vision is living itself and is sustaining itself within and across the entire organization. When the bridges can safely be burnt, and there is no way back then the momentum for success has been achieved.

New processes, quick wins and warm words are only the beginning of what needs to be done to achieve long-term change.

Steps to Build on Change

- Once you have achieved a win, analyze what went right, and what needs improving. PLAN – DO - REVIEW
- Set goals and objectives to continue building on the momentum you've already achieved.
- Look at philosophies such as kaizen, the concept and principle of continuous improvement.
- Keep ideas fresh by developing new champions of change and leaders for your change coalition.

Step 8: Anchor the Changes in Corporate Culture
To make any change stick, it has to become integral to the core of your organization. This is where corporate culture often determines what changes succeed. This is why the values behind your vision must show in day-to-day work.

Leaders have to make continuous efforts to ensure that the

change is seen in every aspect of your organization. This sustainability of change requires a solid place in your organization's culture, and that requires the change you have begun to become anchored inside your organization so it becomes the standard process.

That requires that your company's leaders continue to support the change and celebrate the ability to change. This includes existing staff and new leaders who are brought in. Sustainability through anchoring and embedding is vital otherwise you lose the support of these people

Steps in Anchoring Change:

- Communicate the progress of change every chance you get. Tell success stories about the change process.
- Embed the outcomes of the change into the culture of ideals and values when hiring and training new staff.
- Recognize and reward the key members of your original change coalition, and make sure the rest of the staff remember their contributions.
- Create continuity and succession planning based upon the ability to continue and support that change that has been created. This will help ensure that their legacy is not lost or forgotten.

Kottler's Change Model

Leaders have to work hard to change an organization successfully. When you plan carefully and build the proper foundations, implementing change can be much easier, and you'll improve the chances of success. Too many failures in creating change successfully are caused by either short cutting these processes by saying that they do not need to do each one, or by not resourcing the leadership role enough. If you're too impatient, and if you expect too many results too soon, your plans for change are more likely to fail.

Sustaining Change

As change happens through Kottler's 8-stage model of change so the leaders role in motivating people has to reflect the Kubler-Ross change curve. This curve shows the morale state and how it changes over time as people go through the change process.

Great leadership is about knowing how to support your early adopters (those who get what and why you are making that change) and pre-planning to support them through that stage.

People start with a positive euphoria about change. Then as realization of the magnitude of change required a move to denial and then as things start to change and normality falls apart leading everyone into denial over the possibility of success. At this stage I focus leaders in every field in building a ladder out from denial, from the danger zone of failure. Here is where the quick wins play a vital role in showing progress and that is why the right measurements matter, do not focus on end outcomes but on process improvements.

As people start to see the benefits of change, then they start to experiment with the change that has been made, using it to see how it works rather than wondering if it will work. Somewhere along that experimentation people will make a decision to go with it, do more than experiment but decide to adopt it, and once they have gone there then as they see it works they will decide to integrate the change into how they do whatever the change is they have taken on.

Leadership through change is an important skill primarily in knowing where everyone is along this curve at any time. Knowing where people are enables you as a leader to know how and what to respond with, that supports people as to where they are and moves them forward to the next stage successfully.

The Kubler-Ross change curve

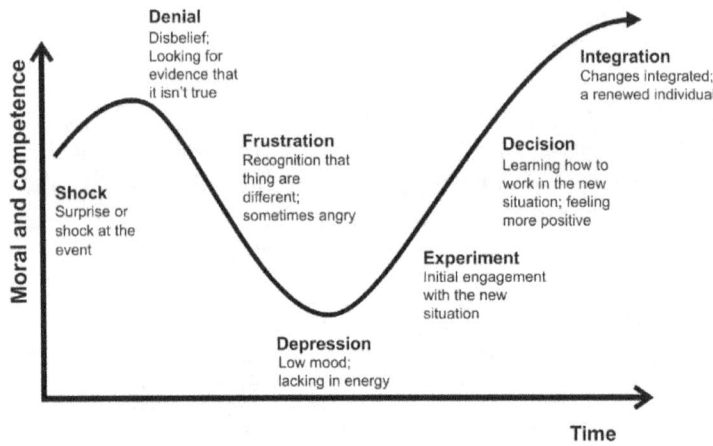

This change model is an important element of working ON your business not IN your business. You are working leading people forward and that is real leadership through change.

Chapter 21   Summary of Making Change

The following is a simple summary of how to make change; this list is an effective summary of the top points.

1. Develop the VISION.
2. Develop the change management plan.
3. Identify critical success factors for change.
4. Understand how people might react.
5. Be prepared for roadblocks.
6. Develop an effective marketing plan.
7. Develop and test the initial change management plan.
8. Adjust the change management plan.
9. Create an atmosphere for success.
10. Celebrate success to embed CHANGE

References:-

- The Power of Why: Simon Sinek TED talk 2009

- Kubler-Ross Change Curve: E. Kubler-Ross (1969) Kubler-Ross Change Curve

- Differences between managers and leaders: Warren Bennis (1985) On Becoming a Leader

- Five-Step Strategy Model: Lafley and Martin's (2013) Five-Step Strategy Model

- Value Chain: Michael Porter's (1985) Competitive Strategy The Value Chain

- The TOWS Matrix: H. Weihrock (1982) The TOWS Matrix: A Tool for Situational Analysis

- Generic Strategies: Michael Porter (1980) Competitive Advantage

- The Bowman Startgeic Clock: Bowman and Faulkner (1996) Bowman's Strategic Clock

- The Change Formula: Beckhard and Harris (1977) with attribution to D. Gleicher.

- 8 Steps in Making Change: John Kottler (1995) Leading Change

www.ingramcontent.com/pod-product-compliance
Lightning Source LLC
Chambersburg PA
CBHW051916170526
45168CB00001B/417